APOCALYPSE

James Keery was born in Coleraine in 1958 and lives in Culcheth, near Warrington. He has published a collection of poems, *That Stranger, The Blues* (1996); edited Burns Singer's *Collected Poems* (2001); and contributed to a number of recent magazines and books, including *PN Review*, *Angel Exhaust* and *Reading Dylan Thomas* (2019).

APOCALYPSE

an anthology

edited by

JAMES KEERY

CARCANET

First published in Great Britain in 2020 by
Carcanet
Alliance House, 30 Cross Street
Manchester M2 7AQ
www.carcanet.co.uk

A CIP catalogue record for this book is
available from the British Library.
ISBN 978 1 78410 818 2

Book design by Andrew Latimer
Printed in Great Britain by SRP Ltd, Exeter, Devon

MIX
Paper from
responsible sources
FSC® C014540

The publisher acknowledges financial
assistance from Arts Council England.

Supported using public funding by
ARTS COUNCIL
ENGLAND

CONTENTS

APOCALYPSE

INTRODUCTION

1. *'Visionary Modernism'*

Apocalypse takes a fresh look at mid-twentieth century British and Irish poetry in English, on the initially disorientating premise that the central body of work is that of Dylan Thomas.

His mid-century career began with a sensation. In 1933, 'The force that through the green fuse', a poem in a sports journal by a provincial teenager, sent shock waves through literary London – acclaim which, as William Empson noted, 'does some credit to the town'. *Apocalypse* is a seismograph of his influence, but it also aims to open long perspectives.

The title signals both. *The New Apocalypse*, conceived in 1938 and published in 1940, edited by J.F. Hendry and Henry Treece, was the first of three anthologies produced by a group which formed around the impact crater of Thomas's poetry. The specific source of the name was a reference by Elizabeth Bowen, in 1937, to 'the apocalyptic writing of Dylan Thomas'.

In the longer perspective, however, the title looks beyond the Apocalyptic anthologies and the immediate period. In the correspondence of the original plotters, Dorian Cooke and John Goodland, the trail leads back, through Henry Miller, to *Apocalypse* by D.H. Lawrence. Criticism has increasingly insisted on the intrinsically apocalyptic aspects of modernism itself, from 'The Second Coming' by W.B. Yeats and the urban apocalypse at the heart of *The Waste Land* to the cynical prescience of Wyndham Lewis in the roaring Twenties: 'Oh it is a wild life that we live in the near West, between one apocalypse and another!' Critics of the Thirties also invariably record a sense of apocalypse as characteristic of the epoch.

Yet there is a distinction to be drawn between the familiar *ironic modernism*, epitomised by W.H. Auden, and an alternative vein of *visionary modernism*. In T.S. Eliot's *New Criterion*, in 1927, a reviewer speaks of 'a vision that is apocalyptic in its embrace of ultimate things'; whilst Edith Sitwell's amusing remark to Gertrude Stein, in 1926, that 'everything in *The New Criterion* is regarded as a newer and more important Apocalypse', illustrates both strains at once. This distinction produces a more coherent alignment of the poets of the Thirties and Forties than conventional distinctions between the classical and the neo-romantic styles, and between the decades as typified by Auden and Thomas. As much a poet of the Thirties as Auden, Thomas published his first collection in the first half of the decade, alongside George Barker and David Gascoyne, also often considered to be quintessentially poets of the Forties.

Contrariwise, Auden's *ironic* modernism has its *visionary* moments ('The Witnesses', 1933):

The sky is darkening like a stain,
Something is going to fall like rain
And it won't be flowers.

As apocalyptic as Bob Dylan's, this hard rain is forecast by the 'witnesses' of Revelation 11. Like Auden, Louis MacNeice writes apocalyptic poems, such as 'Prayer Before Birth', on a theme all but copyrighted by Thomas; but Stephen Spender *became* an Apocalyptic poet, revising 'that day's doom', in a poem of 1938, to 'Apocalypse'; editing an anthology entitled *Young Men Shall See Visions* for Hodder and Stoughton (advertised in the *TLS*, though never released, the title an apocalyptic prophecy from the Book of Acts); and publishing one of the classics of the style, *Ruins and Visions*, in 1942. In a scintillating piece in the Apocalyptic annual,

Transformation (1945), written amidst the onslaught of the doodlebugs, Spender places the 'newest school of English poets' in the context of three generations of modernists:

> The immense resources of all the governments of the world are now being devoted to producing surrealist effects. Surrealism has ceased to be fantasy, its 'objects' hurtle round our heads... The youngest and newest school of English poets signified this... by calling themselves 'apocalyptics'. Instead of being prophets, they were now witnesses in a world... taken over by prophecies... *The Waste Land*, the Revolution, the 'explosion of mania'... and the disintegration, have become part of reality.

The distinction between ironic and visionary modernism might also explain the exclusion of one of the best-loved poems of WWII, 'Naming of Parts' by Henry Reed. Who would change a word of it? Apocalyptic, however, it is not. Amusing poems may have gained admittance – even 'black truth' may 'have a lighter side', as Blanaid Salkeld says – but it is fair to say that humour is not the keynote of the anthology. 'Eternity's extreme unction', as Burns Singer calls it, can be hard to take, but (im)mortality, chief amongst the 'grander themes' proscribed by Kingsley Amis in 1955, is almost definitive of visionary modernism. 'Immortal ordinariness – is that / A meaning you can have?' (Norman MacCaig). Whatever the answer to that one, no Apocalyptic poet would be likely to subscribe to Philip Larkin's conscientious disclaimer, a touchstone for the Movement and its critical heritage: 'We are not suited to the long perspectives / Open at each instant of our lives'. In the face of the aplomb with which such influential figures tend to speak on our behalf, it seems reasonable to suggest a counter-generalisation: that Apocalyptic poets are, if not 'suited', with that subtle implication, then at least 'open' to 'the long perspectives' of which the Movement poets go in fear.

In explicit reaction against the Auden generation (like the Apocalyptic manifesto itself), Gascoyne improvises his own manifesto of visionary modernism, in a journal entry dating from 1938, on 'new poetry from Fabers' by Auden, Spender and MacNeice:

> I feel the existence of a great gap between their generation's conception of poetry and my own… Poetry is… not rhetoric,… nor is it argument or reportage… The tradition of modern English poetry is… quite different from the tradition of Hölderlin, Rimbaud, Rilke, Lorca, Jouve. – I belong to Europe before I belong to England.

This is exactly the context in which this distinction was first drawn by A.T. Tolley in *The Poetry of the Forties* (1985):

> European modernism had little influence on the development of poetry in England… [I]f we characterise Surrealism and the type of writing out of which it grew as 'visionary' modernism (in contrast with the 'ironic' Anglo-American modernism) we can see the poetry of Barker, Thomas and Gascoyne as being in that stream.

Where the stream flows is illustrated, in her own words, by Rosemary Tonks:

> I have developed a visionary modern lyric, and, for it, an idiom in which I can write lyrically, colloquially, and dramatically [about] city life… its anguish, its enraged excitement, its great lonely joys.

Included as a wildcard in Larkin's *Oxford Book of Twentieth Century English Verse* (to his eternal credit), Tonks insists – invoking Rimbaud – on the 'duty of the poet… to excite – to send the senses reeling'. Her own poems have been duly restored to the modernist mainstream by Anthony Rudolf: 'They seem… to have bypassed the Movement poetry of the 1950s and to have emerged from the 1940s poetic matrix of Nicholas Moore, George Barker and J.F. Hendry, poets she would have read in her early 20s'. In fact, as a teenager, in the late Forties, Tonks actually participated in the legendary counterculture, frequenting the Soho pubs and clubs and broadcasting on the BBC. The excitement of one strain of visionary modernism is encapsulated in a stanza from 'Running Away' (see p. 360):

Like some Saint whose only blasphemy is a
Magnificent juice vein that plucks his groin
With April's coarse magicianship as green
As the jade squirt of fruit, I was the child whose breast
Rocks to a muscle savage as Africa.

In the wider perspective, it is revealing to zoom out from Tonks, via Hendry, to Paul Celan, whose Forties poetry parallels, whilst never meeting, the poetry of the Apocalypse:

Green as mould is the house of oblivion.
Before each of the blowing gates your beheaded minstrel turns
blue.
For you he beats his drum made of moss and of harsh pubic hair;
With a festering toe in the sand he traces your eyebrow.
Longer he draws it than ever it was, and the red of your lip.
You fill up the urns here and nourish your heart.

'Sand from the Urns', published in 1948, is drawn from the same well as 'Europe: 1939' by Hendry, which appeared in the second Apocalyptic anthology, *The White Horseman*, in 1941:

Thunder and the blood shout fight to the head in a dream;

Rat seed and strangle harvests in the burning shadows
Where our arteries of wire shroud weed for squinting limbs
And a lopped head, held up like a heart, crushed root and bloody
Brandishes strands of flesh, the fruit of a coughing womb.

Many refugee poets of Central and Eastern Europe made common cause with the Apocalyptic movement. In 1945, Charles Wrey Gardiner's Grey Walls Press published *New Road 1945*, a 200-page hardback edited by Fred Marnau, a Slovakian writing in German and contributor of a story to the third anthology, *The Crown and the Sickle*. He produced an admirable issue. A British contingent, including Moore, Herbert Read, David Wright and Denise Levertoff (as the young English nurse then spelled her name), appears alongside Czech contemporaries, including František Halas and future Nobel prize-winner Jaroslav Seifert, and the illustrious dead of several nations, including Georg Trakl and Stefan George. In 'The Song of Lazarus', Alex Comfort, another Apocalyptic poet, commemorates the Jewish dead with something of the dark irony of 'Todesfuge' (written by 1945, it would not have been out of place); whilst Celan's image of 'black milk' is startlingly anticipated by the teenage Dorian Cooke, in 1938: 'rough and thick / Is black milk… pulled in quarts from a leper's skins'. Celan is known to have taken bearings from Thomas's conception of image-seeds, as well he might. Lines that sound like an out-take from *Sprachgitter* (1959) were written by Thomas, aged fifteen, in 1930:

You shall not let go;
Chain the strong voice
And grip the inexorable song,
Or throw it, stone by stone,
Into the sky.

II. *'Interfluentiality'*

From September 1940 to May 1941, from Exeter to Aberdeen, and from Hull to Belfast, 'hail and fire mingled with blood' were 'hurled down' upon the land, as in the Book of Revelation. In the film *Armageddon*, the NASA chief interrupts a hysterical physicist to simplify the outlook for mankind: 'Basically the worst bits of the Bible'. The Luftwaffe sustained a bombardment of London to which Churchill 'foresaw no end but a demolition of the whole metropolis'. In the aftermath of terrible raids, Dylan Thomas returned to Swansea, and Larkin to Coventry, each to find the city of his birth devastated almost beyond recognition. WWII was the all-too-accurately envisaged end of the period 'between one apocalypse and another', and an apter term than 'Apocalyptic' for the poetry of the age could hardly have been found.

Yet the 'womb of war' in which Thomas's poetry was conceived was not that of WWII, but of WWI, beginning in the year of his birth (the theme of 'I dreamed my genesis'). Broadcast just days after Attlee had put bread on the ration to feed starving Germans, Thomas's 1946 BBC radio talk on Wilfred Owen is as topical as it is Apocalyptic. Thomas presents Owen not only as a socialist prophet, but, first and foremost, as an experimental modernist:

> It's no use trying to imagine what would have happened to Owen had he lived on... Owen alive now, at the age of fifty-three, and half the world starving... We know that... he would always be experimenting technically, deeper and deeper driving towards the final intensity of language... [and] would never have ceased to influence the work of his contemporaries. Had he lived, English poetry would not be the same... Even so, he is one of the four most profound influences upon the poets who came after him; the

other three being Gerard Manley Hopkins, the later W.B. Yeats, and T.S. Eliot.

Thomas's refusal to imagine 'Owen alive now' is also a self-portrait. His influence 'upon the poets who came after him' is unmistakable, but often involves mediations, feedback loops and confluences of influence as intricate as the Book of Kells; whilst the sources of his own *interfluential* poetry, to borrow a word from gospel scholars, are equally intriguing. Look at a cento of 'the verse extracts from *The Plumed Serpent*' by Lawrence, which Thomas was reading 'for the hundredth time' in 1933:

> Child of the living dead, the dead that live,
> Man is a column of blood, with a voice in it.
> The hair of night is dark over our faces.
> Follow me now up the ladder of sparks.
> The Son on the Cross cried out to the dark sun,
> Am I always and only dead, but bone on a Cross of bone?

– and at one from another of his talismans, *Finnegans Wake* by James Joyce –

> He points the deathbone and the quick are still.
> Pariah, cannibal Cain, I who oathily forswore
> The womb that bore you and the paps I sucked,
> Babbling, bubbling, as happy as the day is wet.
> He lifts the lifewand and the dumb speak.

Look, with John Goodby's eyes, at the first poem in the book, by John Masefield, then at 'Before I knocked' and 'The force that through the green fuse'; and at the template for the celebrated line, 'After the first death, there is no other' ('A Refusal to Mourn'), from *The Bombed Happiness* by Hendry: 'That was the first death. There were many others' (turned right side out again by Fader Coram in the BBC production of *His Dark Materials* by Philip Pullman: 'That was the first death. There will be others'). Hendry's 'bad (or rather good) imitations of Dylan Thomas' drew immediate and sustained fire, yet Thomas himself found inspiration in them; and also, for this seminal line, in 'the second death' of the Apocalypse, the lake of fire or Christian Hell (Revelation 20), of which he makes a further, magnificent refusal. Meanwhile, the distinctive rhetorical structure ('Never until… Shall I'), and the salience of 'Majesty' as the first item of a solemn collocation, derive from the final lines of Antonia White's 'Epitaph' (1937), which Thomas had been 'trying to remember… for years' when it was reprinted, shortly before he wrote his own poem, in *New Road 1944* (see p. 65).

In acknowledging Eliot as 'the centre of the cyclone of the modern apocalypse', Ted Hughes makes, in his choice of word, a simultaneous gesture of restitution. How much of Hughes's rewiring of English nature poetry is implicit in that single electrifying line, 'The force that through the green fuse drives the flower'? The visionary modernism of the mid-century, but also of the 'modern apocalypse' in its entirety, is epitomised by the poem which made Dylan Thomas the talk of the town. Yet it is also an elegy for 'the fallen blood', a variation on Owen's 'pushing up daisies' – one of Hopkins's exploding tropes. An anthology could be made of cover versions of this poem alone, beginning with a Blitz update by Kenneth Gee ('Spring, 1941'): 'Spring pushes up the crocus / Like an incendiary fin'. In this long perspective, the best account of the impact of Thomas is by Roy Fisher, born in the same year as Hughes, explaining how, at the end of the Forties, 'reading Thomas… enabled me to start':

> It was like one of those astronomical events where a body is struck by another and kicked out of its familiar orbit into a new one, by

way of a violent wobble. I came across *The Burning Baby*, then read, along with the gang of surrealist and neo-romantic things I was hunting out, the first two collections of poems and *The Map of Love*. It was simply the spectacle of something apparently quite primal (allowing for the obvious tropes and tricks), a sort of linguistic/ imaginative magma, unsuspected innards, the breaking of taboos one hadn't known existed.

Numerous poets of the mid-century were similarly 'entangled in the undergrowth of *Poetry Quarterly* and *Poetry London*', in Larkin's rueful phrase. 'To the hawk on fire… in a whack of wind' ('Over Sir John's Hill') sounds more like Hughes than Thomas, but Hughes's entanglement goes beyond such immediate debts. The 'Orgy and hosannah' of 'distracting devils' at the climax of 'Thrushes' verge on the parodic, yet Thomas is not its principal source. 'For Those Who Are Alive' by Eithne Wilkins reveals image-clusters and a train of thought too idiosyncratically alike to be coincidental (see p. 190). 'Hawk Roosting', another icon, has an obvious precursor in 'The Buzzard' by Kathleen Raine (*Outposts*, 1952):

My task is to scan
The ground and the green
For the small and the animate.
On them I fall
Nor must I fail
My work is to tear
My prey and devour.

Celebrated as a Blakean mystic, Raine's best known poem, 'Envoi', is deceptively gentle:

Take of me what is not my own,
my love, my beauty, and my poem –
the pain is mine, and mine alone.

No sign here of the daemonic poet who suffered lifelong guilt after cursing her beloved under a rowan tree, with devastating results, nor of the 'heart' so balefully described in a poem after Hughes's own ('Storm', *The Pythoness*, 1952):

God in me is the fury on the bare heath…
Raging in the shelterless landscape of the mind
Outside the barred doors of my Goneril heart.

The signature poem, 'The Thought Fox', with which Hughes completed his apprenticeship in 1952 (and duly signed at the bottom right: 'The page is prinTED'), takes its opening line, 'I imagine this midnight moment's forest', from a sonnet by Treece, in his first Faber collection, *Invitation and Warning* (1942): 'Stars shook… and heaved a sigh that I / Should in that midnight minute shout / A song'. There is an equally striking prolepsis of Hughes in Thomas Blackburn's image, in 'Pasiphae' (1953), of the witch-queen 'Blasted and burnt out like a terminal'; and for all its own debt to Thomas, 'Snowdrop' owes much to 'Now in the Time of This Mortal Life' by Norman Nicholson, from the Apocalyptic annual, *New Road 1943*:

Frost is tight upon the land
Constricts it with a bony hand,
Yet with blade as sharp as a nail
The immanent crocus drills the soil.

Imagined as Vikings with a 'fistful of splintered weapons', Hughes's 'Thistles' had a recent ancestor in Laurie Lee's 'Thistle', a 'blue bunch of daggers / rattling upon the wind'; whilst 'The Edge of Day', with 'electric larks' and 'crows, like clinkers', is a nightmare premonition of the Hughesian universe: 'my huge eye a chaos is / Where molten worlds are born' (see p. 193). In *Gaudete* (aka *Under Blood Wood*), 'The lark sizzles in my ear / Like a fuse', with another feedback loop in the distillation of the atomic poetry of Edith Sitwell (see p. 39):

I stepped into the wind
Which entered the tunnel of fire [...]
I saw the snowflake crucified
Upon the nails of nothing.

I heard the atoms praying
To enter his kingdom,
To be broken like bread
On a dark sill, and to bleed.

Sitwell's indebtedness to Thomas is notorious, his to her less rehearsed; yet in her 'Prelude to a Fairy-Tale' (1927), he found an image-seed for no less a poem than 'A Refusal to Mourn': 'The humble Eden of a drop of dew'. Sitwell's metaphor and biblical name inspire the first, whilst her cadence and syntax inform the second of the wartime images in which Thomas pays tribute to the Jewish dead: 'the round / Zion of the water bead / And the synagogue of the ear of corn' (and 'the dew of creation' occurs in a draft). The loop is completed by the exact replication of the second of these lines in 'Flute Notes from a Reedy Pond' by Sylvia Plath:

The moults are tongueless that sang from above the water
Of golgotha at the tip of a reed,
And how a god flimsy as a baby's finger
Shall unhusk himself and steer into the air.

Plath's account of her own 'vision of the apocalypse' resonates with each of these concerns:

> I am not gifted with the tongue of Jeremiah, though I may be sleepless enough before my vision of the apocalypse. My poems do not turn out to be about Hiroshima, but about a child forming itself finger by finger in the dark.

A live wire in American poetry, plundering Hart Crane ('brother-thief of time'; 'voltage of blown blood and vine') and ghost-writing *Homage to Mistress Bradstreet* by John Berryman ('O all your ages at the mercy of my loves / together lie at once, forever or / so long as I happen'; cf. Fern Hill: 'Time let me play and be / Golden in the mercy of his means', and 'Twenty-Four Years': 'I advance for as long as forever is'), Thomas is credited by John Wain with inaugurating, in 'the excitement of a reading… in Oxford' in 1947, the vogue for US formalists such as Richard Wilbur, a crucial stimulus to the Movement itself. Meanwhile, in St Lucia, Derek Walcott, aged eighteen, entitles his privately printed first collection, *Twenty-five Poems* (1948), after Thomas's second. 'As John to Patmos' is a stand-out poem. Yet even the most flagrantly Apocalyptic transmits no sense of the *anxiety*, rather of the *exhilaration* of influence: 'Young as the water I was once, and time tame as wax / Melted my braggart sun'.

For one more example of interfluentiality, take Glyn Jones, whose 1939 poem, 'Night' (see p. 78), is amongst the purest derivatives of Thomas's style. It was Jones, in turn, who told Thomas the tale of Dr William Price, an eccentric Chartist Druid, who burnt the body of an illegitimate son of his old age on a Welsh hillside; acquitted of manslaughter, he legitimised the rite of cremation and inspired the controversial story, 'The Burning Baby'. From Jones's own story, 'Porth-y-rhyd' (1938), Hugh MacDiarmid took the 'found poem', 'Perfect', supplying only the first line. Finally, allowing for the influence of Lawrence on both, 'Esyllt Ferch Brychan' ('Iseult daughter of Brychan'), featured in the Faber anthology *Modern Welsh Poetry* in 1944 and read on air by Thomas in January 1946 (see p. 77), is the source of the banging door as a symbol of joy in Larkin's Apocalyptic 'Wedding Wind' (September 1946), an annunciation of immortality:

The wind blew all my wedding-day,
And my wedding-night was the night of the high wind;
And a stable door was banging, again and again…
Can it be borne, this bodying-forth by wind
Of joy my actions turn on, like a thread
Carrying beads? Shall I be let to sleep
Now this perpetual morning shares my bed?
Can even death dry up
These new delighted lakes, conclude
Our kneeling as cattle by all-generous waters?

III. *'The Awful British New Romantics'*

There were seven poets in *The New Apocalypse*, published by the Fortune Press in 1940. *The White Horseman*, published by Herbert Read at Routledge in 1941, added three more. It was Read, in the *Listener* in 1942, who rebranded the movement as New Romanticism, whilst Grey Walls published *Lyra*, out of series, but edited by two other Apocalyptic poets, the same year. Then, in 1944, *The Crown and the Sickle* appeared from Staples Press, the third and final Apocalyptic anthology by the original editors, with eleven new poets amongst the contributors. All twenty-one poets in the three official Apocalyptic anthologies are included here.

Apocalypse also includes more poets of the neo-romantic diaspora than any since *The New British Poets*, edited by Kenneth Rexroth for New Directions in 1949. For sixty years after that, Apocalyptic poetry was derided and eclipsed. In 1988, John Heath-Stubbs deplored 'the habit of using… "apocalyptic" in an implied pejorative sense as a comprehensive term with which to dismiss almost all the poets of my generation'. The Forties sneer is perhaps, at last, subsiding, but listen to Michael Hofmann, introducing W.S. Graham to American readers, as recently as 2018: 'the 1940s and '50s… strike me as… two rank bad decades for poetry… [I]t was the time of the awful British New Romantics, but really, almost everything and everyone was awful then'. The great majority of those 'awful British New Romantics' are within.

The Apocalyptic anthologies include poets with secure reputations, such as Thomas, MacCaig and Vernon Watkins. However, with exceptions, such as G.S. Fraser and Nicholas Moore, most of the contributors, including Hendry, Treece, Cooke and Comfort, have been overlooked ever since. And so with the Forties as a period: alongside household names such as Barker, Gascoyne, Graham or Sitwell, there are poets whose neo-romantic work will come as a revelation to most readers, including Seán Rafferty, Nessie Dunsmuir and Julian Orde.

This is an anthology of the mid-twentieth century. The first poem, by Masefield, dates from 1910; and the latest, 'Breath' by Nicholas Moore, was written not long before his death in 1986. Yet all but 20 of the 330 poems included were written within fifteen years of the mid-point of the century, between 1935 and 1965; just under 200 date from the decade 1940–1949; and all but the last few contributors were still, or already, writing during the Forties.

Similarly, the focus is on British and Irish poets, with very little geographical latitude. Born in India, Lawrence Durrell spent less time in these islands than almost any other contributor – and was indeed debarred from UK citizenship in 1962 – but who could be more British than *The Durrells* of ITV fame? On the other hand, I have included a number of poets on the grounds of long residence (such as H.D. and Shake Keane), or of British or Irish birth (such as P.K. Page and Wilfred Watson). Naturally, I have also been guided in my selection by other considerations, including space and cost, but the one essential credential is poetic.

Long suits might have been drawn from Yeats, Eliot, Edwin Muir and Basil Bunting, to name four. 'Altarwise by owl-light', 'Little Gidding' and 'The Nightfishing', entire; half of *In Parenthesis*; a dozen of Norman MacCaig's later poems; several by Walter de la Mare, Stevie Smith – and other poets of renown – all belong in the book, but in their celebrity will scarcely be missed. I have been after the best, but have opted, other things being equal, for the less familiar. Most of the poems have not been anthologised since the mid-century, if at all. Other anthologies feature more *poets* than *poems* to be found in *Apocalypse*. I include over thirty of the fifty poets in M.J. Tambimuttu's pioneer anthology, *Poetry in Wartime*, published by Faber in 1942, but only ten poems; and fifty-odd of the seventy poets in Rexroth's classic, but only eighteen poems. Similarly, Jane Dowson's *Women's Poetry of the 1930s*, Anne Powell's *Shadows of War* and Catherine Reilly's *Chaos of the Night* supply only ten poems between them, but it was less painful to omit 'Thinking of War' by Naomi Mitchison from the first, 'April Blitz' by Pauline Rice ('When will there come an end / to the breaking of air, of starry air?'), reprinted in the second from *Poetry London* No. 10, or 'The Munition Workers' by Diana James from the third, because of the availability of these superb anthologies. For the sheer quantity of the poetry of the period, so intemperately held against it, is one of its fascinations. Take *Poetry London* No. 10, 'an anthology of poems by unknown writers', 'the most exciting number to edit'. Omitting all fifty in *Poetry in Wartime*, and even all previous contributors to his magazine, Tambimuttu still finds over ninety new poets, amongst them a dozen featured here (notably a disgruntled Faber reject, R.S. Thomas, whose set of six includes 'A Peasant') and another dozen who might well have been – in search, as always, in his own memorable words, of 'New Blood – The Future – Time materialising'.

ACKNOWLEDGEMENTS

In editing this anthology, I have met with co-operation, and indeed generosity, at almost every turn, from poets, publishers, agents, executors, librarians and archivists. The Writers, Artists and Their Copyright Holders (WATCH) database curated by David Sutton at Reading University has been an invaluable resource. I would also like to thank my friends, Steve Clark, Melinda Derry, Andrew Duncan, John Goodby, Giles Goodland, Panna Grady and Kevin Nolan, and my family, Julie, Jenny and Jack.

The publishers gratefully acknowledge permission to reproduce copyright poems, for which all rights are reserved by the copyright holders:

Bloodaxe Books: James Berry, Roy Fisher (also to Sukey Fisher and Peter Robinson), Denise Levertov (also to New Directions), Bernard Spencer and Rosemary Tonks.

Curtis Brown: Robert Conquest, Lawrence Durrell, William Empson, Laurie Lee, Bryan Magee and Stephen Spender.

Carcanet Press: Valentine Ackland, Patricia Beer, Norman Cameron, Elizabeth Daryush, Donald Davie, H.D., Robert Graves, Michael Hamburger, John Heath-Stubbs, Hugh MacDiarmid, Sorley MacLean, Edwin Morgan, Julian Orde, Anne Ridler, Burns Singer, C.H. Sisson, Charles Tomlinson, Sylvia Townsend Warner, Vernon Watkins, David Wright and Andrew Young.

Faber and Faber: Ted Hughes, Seán Jennett, David Jones, Philip Larkin, Sylvia Plath and Kathleen Raine.

David Higham: Francis Bellerby, Edmund Blunden, Charles Causley, Roland Gant, Elizabeth Jennings, Emanuel Litvinoff, Louis MacNeice, Norman Nicholson, Robert Payne, John Pudney, Herbert Read, Peter Redgrove, Muriel Spark, Dylan Thomas.

Valentine Ackland: Tanya Stobbs. Kingsley Amis: The Wylie Agency. Michael Ayrton: Justine Hopkins. George Barker: Elspeth Barker. John Bayliss: Clare Lahiffe. Francis Berry: Scyld Berry. Thomas Blackburn: Julia Blackburn. Alison Boodson: Tom Neville. Brenda Chamberlain: Reuven Jasser. Leonard Clark: Bob Clark. Jack Clemo: Special Collections, University of Exeter. Prunella Clough: Sophie Collins; Estate of Prunella Clough. Alex Comfort: Nicholas Comfort. Tony Connor: the poet. Dorian Cooke: William Cooke. Maurice James Craig: Jonathan Williams. Frances Cornford: Trustees of the Frances Crofts Cornford Will Trust. Anthony Cronin: New Island Books. Ian Davie: Andrew Wilson. Paul Dehn: Berlin Associates. Denis Devlin: Pat Boran and John F. Deane. Silvia Dobson: Beinecke Rare Book and Manuscript Library, Yale University. Nessie Dunsmuir: Anthony Astbury. Ian Fletcher: Loraine Fletcher. G.S. Fraser: George Fraser. Christopher Fry: Max Vickers. Roy Fuller: John Fuller. Robert Garioch: Morag Sutherland. David Gascoyne: Estate of David Gascoyne; Stephen Stuart-Smith. Sydney Goodsir Smith: Alma Books. W.S. Graham: Estate of W.S. Graham; Rosalind Mudaliar. Robert Greacen: Arethusa Greacen and John F. Deane. J.C. Hall: Shoestring Press. Peter Hellings: Pontefract Press. Hamish Henderson: Janet Henderson. J.F. Hendry: Robert Calder. John Hewitt: Keith Millar.

Geoffrey Hill: Jeremy Hill. John Holloway: The Syndics of Cambridge University Library. Emyr Humphreys: Siôn Humphreys and the poet. Daniel Huws: the poet. Glyn Jones: Ruth Stephens. Patrick Kavanagh: Jonathan Williams. Francis King: Vickie Dillon and A.M. Heath. James Kirkup: South Shields Library. John Knight: Andy Ching. Susanne Knowles: Orion Publishing Group. Freda Laughton: Emma Penney. Patrick Leigh Fermor: Aitken Alexander. Edward Lowbury: Ruth Lowbury. Malcolm Lowry: Sterling Lord Literistic. Mina Loy: Roger Conover. Norman MacCaig: Ewen MacCaig and Birlinn Books (it is acknowledged that the poet 'disowned' his Forties poetry as being 'overly obscure, if not incomprehensible'). Donagh MacDonagh: Brenda MacDonagh. Roy McFadden: Grania McFadden. George Mackay Brown: John Murray. John Masefield: The Society of Authors as the Literary Representative of the Estate of John Masefield. Roland Mathias: Glyn Mathias. Joseph Macleod: Iain A. Macleod. Christopher Middleton: Sheep Meadow Press. Nicholas Moore: The Syndics of Cambridge University Library. Hubert Nicholson: Eileen Nicoll. Barbara Norman: Tuba Press. Philip O'Connor: Felix O'Connor and Panna Grady. John Ormond: Rian Evans. P.K. Page: The Porcupine's Quill Press. Mervyn Peake: Peters, Fraser, Dunlop. Ruth Pitter: Mark Pitter. F.T. Prince: Rosanna Salbashian. Seán Rafferty: Christian Coupe. James Reeves: Michael Irwin. Keidrych Rhys: Angharad Rhys. I.A. Richards: R. Luckett. Lynette Roberts: Angharad Rhys. W.R. Rodgers: Gallery Press. John Rodker: Ian Patterson. Alan Rook: Michael Rook. Francis Scarfe: Bruno Scarfe. Tom Scott: Joy Hendry. E.J. Scovell: Catherine Buffonge. Jon Silkin: Jon Glover. Edith Sitwell: Peters, Fraser, Dunlop. Robin Skelton: Alison Skelton. Elizabeth Smart: HarperCollins. Derek Stanford: Pan Macmillan. Adrian

Stokes: Telfer Stokes. Randall Swingler: Judith Williams. R.S. Thomas: Orion Publishing Group. Terence Tiller: Todd Swift. Sylvia Townsend Warner: Tanya Stobbs. Henry Treece: Johnson and Alcock. Eugene Watters: Rita Kelly. Antonia White: Andrew Chitty. Sheila Wingfield: David Pryce-Jones. George Woodcock: Black Rose Books. Gamel Woolsey: Stéphane Corre.

Every effort has been made to trace copyright holders, but any who have been overlooked are welcome to contact the publishers, who will be pleased to make the necessary arrangements.

POEMS

JOHN MASEFIELD [1878–1967]

C.L.M.

In the dark womb where I began
My mother's life made me a man.
Through all the months of human birth
Her beauty fed my common earth.
I cannot see, nor breathe, nor stir,
But through the death of some of her.

Down in the darkness of the grave
She cannot see the life she gave.
For all her love, she cannot tell
Whether I use it ill or well,
Nor knock at dusty doors to find
Her beauty dusty in the mind.

If the grave's gates could be undone,
She would not know her little son,
I am so grown. If we should meet
She would pass by me in the street,
Unless my soul's face let her see
My sense of what she did for me.

What have I done to keep in mind
My debt to her and womankind?
What woman's happier life repays
Her for those months of wretched days?
For all my mouthless body leeched
Ere Birth's releasing hell was reached?

What have I done, or tried, or said
In thanks to that dear woman dead?
Men triumph over women still,
Men trample women's rights at will,
And man's lust roves the world untamed.

***

O grave, keep shut lest I be shamed.

Neville Chamberlain

As Priam to Achilles for his son,
So you, into the night, divinely led,
To ask that young men's bodies, not yet dead,
Be given from the battle not begun.

BLANAID SALKELD [1880–1959]

Radio Train

Not the loud train
Praises the bright, bright, girls, with the fine
Curtains of rain
Blowing about them, along the line –
Making the swift passage
Of bog and rocks, sparkling and tender –
Nor any message
Of the dissolved heavens' surrender:
To the low, far

Hills stooping, in pelican homage –
As on an altar,
Piling sacrifice of their plumage.
It takes discernment
Of the human heart, in discipline
Of will's internment,
To surmise lightnings of the divine.
Pale, fierce flower
With glory of red-gold foliage –
Mocking this power,
She is in no humour to engage –
Various
As this autumn day – splendid and dim,
In a frowning fuss
Shrugs – or smiles a moment's peace at him.
But, to my right,
Loftier beauty lurks – silent, deep –
Not so bright,
Calm as death, and perfect as its sleep.
I would search where
Mighty statues of great Capitals
Crouch, stand, outstare
Dark and days of snows and cuckoo-calls –
Seeking the rare
Depth of spirit up-shadowing slow
Into that calm stare,
I bear ever with me, as I go.
Bright girls' image,
All set within: and the noisy train –
The stooped skies' plumage
On low, far hills – and the closer rain.
Still – slow spreading
Browns and greys: by road to Carraroe:
Fine, fine rains treading

These holy colours down, as we go.
Journey without end –
Immortal fragment; but to remain,
A ready friend,
Softening night's wrath and day's disdain.

Equity

Now I must leave my airy loft… to stand
Before my own harsh judgment – and decide
How far the accounts I kept were falsified –
My punishment to come from the cold hand
Of equity, no voice will countermand.
My life is forfeit, if these figures lied.
But – may black truth not have a lighter side?
Lifting my light pack, what if I abscond?
I'll face my trial, though – blinded, fear-frozen.
There is a charity, too wise for pity –
May blow in through the windows of a court –
Wrecking the evidence – a mere spoil-sport –
Scattering these woes that press past all entreaty –
Leaving me with the happiness I had chosen.

MINA LOY [1882–1966]

Aviators' Eyes

Among us
Aviators' eyes
never efface their far focus

A stark line
of vigil
crosses the all-aerial outlook
of the iris

Aviators' eyes
have indrawn the horizon
of drifting heaven

Aviators' eyes
on arrow excursion
into profusion of distance
beyond our residence,

fly an illusion of unmoving motion
into dissolving fortresses of cloud,
intrude upon the jewel of the rainbow,

return here from the breathless stratosphere.

Aviators'
eyes of survival.

ANDREW YOUNG [1885–1971]

Reflections on the River

Rose-petals fall without a touch
As though it were too much
I should be standing by,
And poplars in no wind at all
Keep swaying left and right
With the slow motion of their height
Beneath a small white cloud that soon
Will pluck light from the dark and be the moon.

But where roach rise and bite the Ouse
Round ripples spread out like the first
Drops of a storm about to burst
And in the water toss the boughs
And crack the garden wall;
And as I gaze down in the sky
I see the whole vault shake
As though the heavens were seized with an earthquake.

H.D. [1886–1961]

from *R.A.F.*

I

He said, I'm just out of hospital,
but I'm still flying.

I answered, of course,
angry, prescient, knowing

what fire lay behind his wide stare,
what fury of desire

impelled him,
pretending not to notice

his stammer
and that now, in his agony to express himself

his speech failed
altogether,

and his eyes seemed to gather
in their white-heat,

all the fires of the wind,
fire of sleet,

snow like white-fire pellets,
congealed radium, planets

like snow-flakes:
and I thought,

the sun
is only a round platform

for his feet
to rest upon.

II

So I knew his name,
the coming-one

from a far star,
I knew he would come again,

though I did not know
he would come so soon;

he stood by my desk
in my room

where I write this;
he did not wear

his blue tunic with the wings,
nor his cap with the crown;

his flying-helmet,
and his cumbersome trappings

were unfamiliar,
like a deep-sea diver.

III

I had said,
I want to thank you,

he had said,
for what?

I had said,
it is very difficult

to say what I want,
I mean – I want

personally to thank you
for what you have done;

he had said,
I did nothing,

it was the others;
I went on,

for a moment infected with his stammer
but persistent,

I will think of you
when they come over,

I mean – I understand – I know –
I was there the whole time

in the Battle
of Britain.

IV

He came again,
he did not speak;

I thought; he stands by my desk
in the dark,

he is emissary,
maybe he will speak later,

(does he still stammer?)
I remembered

how I had thought
this field, that meadow

is branded for eternity
(whatever becomes of our earth)

with the mark
of the new cross,

the flying shadow
of high wings,

moving
over the grass.

V

Fortunately, there was no time
for lesser intimacy

than this –
instantaneous flash,

recognition, premonition, vision;
fortunately, there was no time,

for the two-edged drawn-swords
of our two separate twin-beings

to dull; no danger of rust;
the Archangel's own fine blade

so neatly divided us,
in the beginning.

VI

He was huddled
in the opposite corner,

bare-headed, curiously slumped forward
as if he were about to fall over;

the compartment was crowded,
I was facing forward;

I said, put your feet up here
and I wedged myself tighter

and dozed off in the roar
and the train rumble.

VII

In the train jolt
our knees brushed

and he murmured, sorry:
he was there;

I knew in the half-daze,
in the drug and drift,

the hypnotic sway
of the train, that we were very near;

we could not have been nearer,
and my mind winged away;

our minds are winged,
though our feet are clay.

[…]

XII

If I dare recall
his last swift grave smile,

I award myself
some inch of ribbon

for valour,
such as he wore,

for I am stricken
as never before,

by the thought
of ineptitude, sloth, evil

that prosper,
while such as he fall.

London,
17th September, 1941

FRANCES CORNFORD [1886–1960]

Soldiers on the Platform

Look how these young, bare, bullock faces know,
With a simplicity like drawing breath,
That out of happiness we fall on woe
And in the midst of life we are in death.

See how in staring sameness each one stands,
His laden shoulders, and his scoured hands;
But each behind his wall of flesh and bone
Thinks with this secret he is armed alone.

Daybreak

I heard an ancient sound: a cock that crew
    In graying light as I lay warm in bed.
A long metallic cry of dung and dew
    And the unearthly dead.

EDWARD THOMPSON [1886–1946]

In Patmos: I

In my exile in Patmos, a slave:
In the drift between day and dusk, when the seas
Were a fire, when the mind was afire:
I John saw these things:
I saw Lucifer fall
Shot down in flames,
Clawed down, his wings
Cleft by a boy – tormented and turning,
They shredded and furled
Till they crashed to the field
That was bought with blood.
In the place of mean streets
Where rejoicing he spread
His gaunt wings,
Where he havocked and killed,
His malice was stilled,
His hurt was fulfilled.
As he lies on Thames mud
Some bird with struck pinion,
So he lay.
I John saw these things.

(What isle shall receive him? What wilderness hide,
For covert and shield
Till his death-wound be healed?
He that for foe has the world –
The world is his grave!)

EDITH SITWELL [1887–1964]

Still Falls the Rain

The Raids, 1940. Night and Dawn

Still falls the Rain –
Dark as the world of man, black as our loss –
Blind as the nineteen hundred and forty nails
Upon the Cross.

Still falls the Rain
With a sound like the pulse of the heart that is changed to the
    hammer-beat
In the Potters' Field, and the sound of the impious feet

On the Tomb:
                    Still falls the Rain
In the Field of Blood where the small hopes breed and the
    human brain
Nurtures its greed, that worm with the brow of Cain.

Still falls the Rain
At the feet of the Starved Man hung upon the Cross.
Christ that each day, each night, nails there, have mercy on us –

On Dives and on Lazarus:
Under the Rain the sore and the gold are as one.

Still falls the Rain –
Still falls the Blood from the Starved Man's wounded Side:
He bears in His Heart all wounds, – those of the light that died,
The last faint spark
In the self-murdered heart, the wounds of the sad uncomprehending dark,
The wounds of the baited bear, –
The blind and weeping bear whom the keepers beat
On his helpless flesh… the tears of the hunted hare.

Still falls the Rain –
Then – O Ile leape up to my God: who pulles me doune –
See, see where Christ's blood streames in the firmament:
It flows from the Brow we nailed upon the tree
Deep to the dying, to the thirsting heart
That holds the fires of the world, – dark-smirched with pain
As Caesar's laurel crown.

Then sounds the voice of One who like the heart of man
Was once a child who among beasts has lain –
'Still do I love, still shed my innocent light, my Blood, for thee'.

ELIZABETH DARYUSH [1887–1997]

Invalid Dawn

Above the grey down
   gather, wan, the glows;
relieved by leaden
   gleams a star-gang goes;

in the dark valley
   here and there enters
a spark, laggardly,
   to the faint watchers

that were there all night –
   factory, station
and hospital light.
   Tired of lamp, star, sun,

bound to my strait bed
   uncurtained, I see
heaven itself law-led,
   earth in slavery.

DOROTHY WELLESLEY [1889–1956]

Mother

Woman, thou shalt say to son:
'I, the blood, got thee upon
Nothing but a phallic stone.
This, no more – a phallic stone.

Now I wait your probable death,
I, who was a fact of earth,
Never held a fainting faith
In Buddha or in Christ's belief.

Life is naught but bitter moan
Got upon an ancient stone'.

Some such curse the woman hath.

HUGH MACDIARMID [1892–1978]

from *On a Raised Beach: To James H. Whyte*

All is lithogenesis – or lochia,
Carpolite fruit of the forbidden tree,
Stones blacker than any in the Caaba,
Cream-coloured caen-stone, chatoyant pieces,
Celadon and corbeau, bistre and beige,
Glaucous, hoar, enfouldered, cyathiform,
Making mere faculae of the sun and moon,
I study you glout and gloss, but have

No cadrans to adjust you with, and turn again
From optik to haptik and like a blind man run
My fingers over you, arris by arris, burr by burr,
Slickensides, truité, rugas, foveoles,
Bringing my aesthesis in vain to bear,
An angle-titch to all your corrugations and coigns,
Hatched foraminous cavo-rilievo of the world,
Deictic, fiducial stones. Chiliad by chiliad
What bricole piled you here, stupendous cairn?
What artist poses the Earth écorché thus,
Pillar of creation engouled in me?
What eburnation augments you with men's bones,
Every energumen an Endymion yet?
All the other stones are in this haecceity it seems,
But where is the Christophanic rock that moved?
What Cabirian song from this catasta comes?

Deep conviction or preference can seldom
Find direct terms in which to express itself.
Today on this shingle shelf
I understand this pensive reluctance so well,
This not discommendable obstinacy,
These contrivances of an inexpressive critical feeling,
These stones with their resolve that Creation shall not be
Injured by iconoclasts and quacks. Nothing has stirred
Since I lay down this morning an eternity ago
But one bird. The widest open door is the least liable to
  intrusion,
Ubiquitous as the sunlight, unfrequented as the sun.

from *In Memoriam James Joyce*

Let the only consistency
In the course of my poetry
Be like that of the hawthorn tree
Which in early Spring breaks
Fresh emerald, then by nature's law
Darkens and deepens and takes
Tints of purple-maroon, rose-madder and straw.

Sometimes these hues are found
Together, in pleasing harmony bound.
Sometimes they succeed each other. But through
All the changes in which the hawthorn is dight,
No matter in what order, one thing is sure
– The haws shine ever the more ruddily bright!
And when the leaves have passed
Or only in a few tatters remain
The tree to the winter condemned
                                    Stands forth at last
          Not bare and drab and pitiful,
But a candelabrum of oxidised silver gemmed
By innumerable points of ruby
Which dominate the whole and are visible
Even at considerable distance
As flame-points of living fire.
That so it may be
With my poems too at last glance
Is my only desire.

All else must be sacrificed to this great cause.
I fear no hardships. I have counted the cost.
I with my heart's blood as the hawthorn with its haws
Which are sweetened and polished by the frost!

[…]

The gold edging of a bough at sunset, its pantile way
Forming a double curve, tegula and imbrex in one,
Seems at times a movement on which I might be borne
Happily to infinity; but again I am glad
When it suddenly ceases and I find myself
Pursuing no longer a rhythm of duramen
But bouncing on the diploe in a clearing between earth and air
Or headlong in dewy dallops or a moon-spairged fernshaw
Or caught in a dark dumosity, or even
In open country again watching an aching spargosis of stars.

Perfect

On the Western Seaboard of South Uist
(Los muertos abren los ojos a los que viven)

I found a pigeon's skull on the machair,
All the bones pure white and dry, and chalky,
But perfect,
Without a crack or a flaw anywhere.

At the back, rising out of the beak,
Were twin domes like bubbles of thin bone,
Almost transparent, where the brain had been
That fixed the tilt of the wings.

SYLVIA TOWNSEND WARNER [1893–1978]

Recognition

But this child was not of wax.
Life was under the mute skin
And still showed red through the cracks.
It is well known that the children of Spain

Were carved cheaply out of wood,
The children of China but yellow leaves on the wind:
This was an English child that lay in the road.
They told me to weep once more, but I found

No tears, and though the mourners then
Threw stones at me in grief's and God's name
I had no blood to quicken for God or man.
For I remembered how to my childhood had come

Hearsay of Justice. Now, overhead,
Rang the inflexible music of her sword;
Blindfold she went over with sure tread.
I knew, and acknowledged her, and adored.

Twelve Poems in the Manner of Bewick: VII

I see they have a vine.
It's small but genuine.
Its leaves can really fall,
Its roots are in a small
Tub that is painted green.

They have a dove-cot too,
And that is painted blue.
It's vacant though commodious,
For doves in time grow odious
That shit as well as coo.

Further, they have a dump
Of sand, a stirrup-pump,
A bucket and a hatchet
And little bags to snatch at
In case of the last trump.

Oh, Bacchus, rowdy youth,
In whose red cup is truth,
O Venus, tranquil nurse
Of scandal and divorce,
Inscribe this house for wrath!

Not terror

Not terror,
Only the wind spreads pallor
Over the fleeing willow-branches, over the river
Thrust backward in its flow.
A year ago
Realisation drove my thoughts just so.

No succour.
You were dying of cancer;
No possible hope, no averting, no answer.
Nothing, but to undergo –
What I did not know.
Rending on rending, throe and the death-throe.

Now, no terror.
You dead, all dreads are over.
Careless, I watch the wind seize on the river;
Into the river I throw
Myself, a yellow
Discarded willow-leaf, and watch the flow
Of my remaindered days dandle me onward –

Whither I know not but surely that I go.

I.A. RICHARDS [1893–1979]

The Strayed Poet: Ludwig Wittgenstein

How salute you, Dubious Angel,
Proud as the proudest in the race of men,
Battler with the deadliest burden
Self can lay on thought to bind a spell.

How compel (what use else in excelling!)
How overcome (though not a trader's inch you'd yield);
Hide (from yourself?) what well must be concealed;
Earn so a destiny awaits its telling.

Assume Yourself: your selves to duty cowing
By the great Act of vanity maintained,
That old presumption, now to reign unreined,
Reckless of what in all you're disallowing.

Round on round through the long decades of guessing
Against a bosom Jacob who prevailed,
Got off with all the questions duly veiled,
Won out – new named – received the Blessing,

Prospered. His spiritual sons sit in our studies,
Teaching talkers commonsense, by screed,
How to cobble a problem when there's need.
Your scions are fewer far – despite those 'Bloody's.

***

Your voice and his I heard in those Non-Lectures
– Hammock chairs sprawled skew-wise all about;
Moore in the armchair bent on writing it all out –
Each soul agog for any word of yours.

Few could long withstand your haggard beauty,
Disdainful lips, wide eyes bright-lit with scorn,
Furrowed brow, square smile, sorrow-born
World-abandoning devotion to your duty.

Such the torment felt, the spell-bound listeners
Watched and waited for the words to come,
Held and bit their breath while you were dumb,
Anguished, helpless, for the hidden prisoners.

Poke the fire again! Open the window!
Shut it! – patient pacing unavailing,
Barren the revelations on the ceiling –
Dash back again to agitate a cinder.

'O it's so clear! It's absolutely clear!'
Tense nerves crisp tenser then throughout the school;
Pencils are poised: *'Oh, I'm a bloody fool!*
A damn'd fool!' – So: however it appear.

Not that the Master isn't pedagogic:
Thought-free brows grow pearly as they gaze.
Hearts bleed with him. But – should you want a blaze,
Try prompting! Who is the next will drop a brick?

Window re-opened, fire attack't again,
(Leave, but leave what's out, long since, alone!)
Great calm; a sentence started; then the groan
Arrests the pencil leads. Round back to the refrain.

***

What withheld, O Will volcanic:
Riven eagle, staring at the Sun?
Sight denied you? Blinded such an One?
What remained you but the drive Satanic?

WHAT MAY NOT BE SAID: you could not say it.
Let all language then turn to a game.
(Jacob, go gently, he's coming into aim)
Worth the candle? No. Why now illuminate?

What the stakes though? Still sidereal.
What there is: 'The World and Life are One'.
Shrivels or grows together all that's done.
Seeing: 'The Eye altering alters All'.

Blake's Eye, exact. But you in your *Tractatus*:
'The limits of my language mean the limits of my world'.
What sets our limits? How were you unfurled?
Where is the Rule assigns to us our status?

'The thinking... subject: there is no such thing'.
'Metaphysical I' instead: 'no part, but limit'.
'My world, the world is'. They much more than fit;
Are one, not two: one single uttering.

So *I* and *my* aren't here our current words,
Live in another language far from ours,
Hardly a language: limitless its powers.
Speech to that WORD – forget not – ill accords.

'Everything that can be said can be said clearly'.
Maybe; with what strained sense for *clear* and *say*?
Those other things that can't, alas, must they
Be 'shown' – by whom and howsoever dearly?

Those picturing facts *Tractatus* wished at us:
Against the new Rules! Nothing to picture now!
No picturers, no pictures! Jacob who would not bow
Can well insist we take it from him thus.

Instead of mirroring – and, far less, comparing –
Let us observe the Rules – not ours to change!
Or are they? Why not think up a range
Of Rules for Rules: up, up... beyond all bearing?

Much turned on who among the YOUs you were.
Some YOUs, it seemed, had wider scope for play.
One YOU, (he limped, that YOU), won *May*;
Others *May not*, for all their zeal and care.

Collector of Blessings, count your gains; earmark
The bleatings; Peniel recall. That face of God
Overcame you not, old trickster, though roughshod
He wrenched your hip, ford-haunting in the dark.

But now you hold the ford, let whom you list,
Pass on the word, taking his name in vain,
Taking the hairy hand, the mask of pain,
The wordlessness that can, so will, insist.

Insist? To whom? The faithful, few but fit;
Or found unfitted – ah, exposed at last,
Void echoers. Beware, poor paraphrast:
Say it *for* me, would you! That I *don't* permit.

Insisting still on what's so clear and sure,
Say as you may, all, all, must get it wrong:
'Not that at all! Good Heavens!' No words strong
Enough even to hint what you endure.

***

Above these little games a Game there plays
Takes note of 'airs' – has much to do with air
(Aeronautical engineers), with the impair,
And some invariants Plato's page displays.

Watching it mutely, an onlooker's neglect
Seemed wiser as well as safer. None could aid.
Much there was here would make the Elect afraid.
Eyes as deject as mine must be suspect.

Fallen to a game, alas, and in despair:
Too heady, too enthralling, such command?
Jacob be given up as deodand.
Let that alone for ever, Prince of the Air.

HERBERT READ [1893–1968]

1945

They came running over the perilous sands
        Children with their golden eyes
Crying: *Look! We have found samphire*
        Holding out their bone-ridden hands.

It might have been the spittle of wrens
        Or the silver nest of a squirrel
For I was invested with the darkness
        Of an ancient quarrel whose omens
Lay scattered on the silted beach.
        The children came running toward me

But I saw only the waves behind them
        Cold, salt and disastrous
Lift their black banners and break
        Endlessly, without resurrection.

JOHN RODKER [1894–1955]

The Searchlight

The searchlights over London
are like the fingers of a woman,
wandering over the dead form of a lover.

She had not thought to do that
while he was living,
to better know his loveliness
or if she had –
he'd stopped her with his kisses –
Now in her great grief
her fingers are to her
sight and sound and hearing.

By all the ways of sense
she knows him lost to her,
yet cannot voice her grief.

Only can she raise white hands towards the heavens
and passionate cursings and great grief,
yet no sign comes, no portent:
O if one blistering tear would come from on high
to crumple up and twist the earth
she'd know her nightly passion not so vain
when her first pang
burst the heavens with howling of guns.

DAVID JONES [1895–1974]

Prothalamion: for M. & H.

At the time of the dooms
in the third quarter of the Reaper's Moon,
in the Island of Britain, in Troy Novaunt,
at the approach of the hateful and evil decision
at about the inception of the last round, toward
the time of the ultimate uncovering – when the
speaking is of no further consequence and naked
mechanism decides who shall be master.

In flame-lap and split masonry,
where the high fires leap and the merchandise
of the merchants, under whatsoever deep
vaulting, rocks now, knows the blast, feels the
unpredictable violence. When the poor, in
ramshackle habitation or flimsy bunk-hole,
apprehend in their innocent bodies horrors
unnamed from the foundation of the world.
When Troy towers are a feeble analogy and
the Harrying of the North a child's tale, when
fear rules and bombast pretends to competence.
Because of the detestable counsel, directly
because of the merchants' rule. When there is
hurrying in the streets (these dive where the
architrave juts – or under any appearance of
cover). At the time of the howling, in the days
of the final desolations, at the precise moment
of the eclipse:
Margaret (gentle as falcon, or
hawk of the tower) with
Harman, my sweet friend

spread in a vault their bed of unity, to mock
the unmaking.

So have I heard bird-song, beneath the
trajectory zone, at Passchendaele, or seen
flowers lean toward each other, under the sun
that shined to delineate the hate and mutilation
of the Forward Area.

written
between 10.30 and midnight on
Thursday, Sept. 12th, 1940,
61 Kings Road Chelsea, SW3
D.J.

LILIAN BOWES LYON [1895–1949]

Daybreak

Morning is a revealing; confession of rivers,
Rainfall hushed of the rhetoric of surprise,
Field that can furrow the heart; a land our eyes
Have learned by rote, not leaned over like lover;

Secret divulged, of towns in a pit of horror,
Wars white-hot in the foundry's flickering womb;
Compassionately day underlines the doom
We paste on a hoarding, peer at in a mirror;

Tripped by the tree's root – all perfection felled
Yet faint with bloom – we flatter in man the torrid
Zealot of metal, cheat the wildwood forehead;
Prune of its wonder the post-Calvary world.

Morning is a redeeming and a condemning.
Sparrows at two a farthing leave no smudge
On sanguine earth! May dawn forbear to judge
Between my blood-guilt and the bomber gleaming.

ROBERT GRAVES [1895–1985]

Through Nightmare

Never be disenchanted of
That place you sometimes dream yourself into,
Lying at large remove beyond all dream,
Or those you find there, though but seldom
In their company seated –

The untameable, the live, the gentle,
Have you not known them? Whom? They carry
Time looped so river-wise about their house
There's no way in by history's road
To name or number them.

In your sleepy eyes I read the journey
Of which disjointedly you tell; which stirs
My loving admiration, that you should travel
Through nightmare to a lost and moated land,
Who are timorous by nature.

Surgical Ward: Men

Something occurred after the operation
To scare the surgeons (though no fault of theirs),
Whose reassurance did not fool me long.
Beyond the shy, concerned faces of nurses
A single white hot eye, focusing on me,
Forced sweat in rivers down from scalp to belly.
I whistled, gasped, or sang, with whitening knuckles
Clutched at my bed grip almost till it cracked:
Too proud, still, to let loose Bedlamite screeches
And bring the charge-nurse scuttling down the aisle
With morphia-needle levelled...

Lady Morphia –

Her scorpion kiss and dark gyrating dreams –
She in mistrust of whom I dared out-dare,
Two minutes longer than seemed possible,
Pain, that unpurposed, matchless elemental
Stronger than fear or grief, stranger than love.

GAMEL WOOLSEY [1895–1968]

The Story Being Ended

The story, being ended, now is clear;
The tragedy concealed in littleness
Shows its sharp bone;
The long dull weariness
Is suddenly revealed for what it was –
The martyrdom.
Saints find the route to heaven
By devious paths;

Sinners can go that leafy road to hell –
Is there a third way through the wilderness?
A way to where the heart went,
Where the past
Is folded closely in a little space;
Back to the done, back to the failed and lost.
(Where was the turning that should not be taken,
What was the price to pay, and at whose cost?)

EDMUND BLUNDEN [1896–1974]

Exorcised

Twenty years had nearly passed since the War called Great had roared
  its last,
And some were talking, men who fought the Somme before their
  twentieth year:
They talked of echoes, shadows, hauntings not so easily exorcised,
They granted Time had healed grim wounds, and yet these watchers
  recognised
    One stubborn and total fear.

'My dreams', said one, and spoke for all, 'less frequently these nights
  recall
The clear-cut circumstance, the countless bitter facts familiar then
In gunpit, shellhole, raid, patrol; the mud that swallowed gun, mule,
  man
Is seldom in my dreaming track, nor aid-post blood that piteous ran,
    Nor the dead in smashed-down den;

But this it is which shatters sleep, and makes one's weary body leap:
Out of the grey uncertain dream this sentence speaks from shore to shore.
"The Armistice has all gone wrong. While we were out of the abyss,
It seemed heaven's mercy, faked you see merely to add new death to this:
The War is on once more'".

Twenty years had nearly passed, and while these watched, they saw aghast
That giant enemy of sleep, that ghost which summed the worst they knew
Come creeping into waking thought, creeping and gathering like a storm
About the summer's loveliness, a vaster, more inhuman form.
The dream was coming true.

Back to your madhouse, child of hell: too many of us know you well.
Infest our sleep, if thence we keep some record of your eyeless eyes.
But trespass not in the face of day. You find you cannot prowl this way;
Your very foulness forearmed those who now have checked your matinée,
The generous, selfless, wise.

How things most complex, coiled and twined, simplicity may best unbind
Is no new secret; but till now it never showed so fountain-clear.
The meeting of four men as friends unhorses all the ancient fiends;
Believing still the best will ever yield the best, as now it ends
One swollen and final fear.

WILLIAM JEFFREY [1896–1946]

Stones

The stones in Jordan's stream
Perceived the dove descend
In its lily of light:
That glory entered
Their interminable dream.

The stones in Edom's wilderness
Observed the fiend
Take five of their number
And build a cairn thereof,
And beckoning to Jesus
He pointed to the stones and said:
Make bread.
But because of his great love
For the uniqueness of created things,
The confraternity in disparity
Of plant and rock, of flesh and wings,
Jesus would not translate the stones
Out of their immobile immortality
Into that dynasty of death,
Decaying bread:

The stones upon Golgotha's hill
Took the shadow of the cross
Upon them like the scorch of ice:
And they felt the flick of dice
And Jesus' blood mingling with his mother's tears;
And these made indelible stains;
And some of them were taken up
And with curses thrown

At that rejected throne,
And others felt the clamorous butts of Roman spears:
And the pity, horror, and love within them pent
Welled out and shook the earth.
And the veil was rent.

The great stones of the tomb
Enfolded Jesus' body
In silence and deep gloom.
They had him to themselves alone,
That shard of him, sinew and bone,
Transient dust on their immortality.
And now their inanimate heart
Yearned over that shrouded form:
And while three midnights passed
They made of that tomb
A womb:

The fragile bones renewed their strength,
The flesh trembled and moved,
The glory of the dove
Re-descended from above,
And with the break of day
The door was rolled away:
The function of the stones was done:
His second birth
Achieved on earth,
Jesus walked into the sun.

RUTH PITTER [1897–1992]

The Bridge

Where is the truth that will inform my sorrow?
I am sure myself that sorrow is not the truth.
These lovely shapes of sorrow are empty vessels
Waiting for wine: they wait to be informed.
Men make the vessels on either side of the river;
On this the hither side the artists make them,
And there over the water the workmen make them:
These frail, with a peacock glaze, and the others heavy,
Simple as doom, made to endure the furnace.
War shatters the peacock-jars: let us go over.

Indeed we have no choice but to go over.

There is always a way for those who must go over:
Always a bridge from the known to the unknown.
When from the known the mind revolts and despairs
There lies the way, and there we must go over.

O truth, is it death there over the river,
Or is it life, new life in a land of summer?
The mind is an empty vessel, a shape of sorrow,
Fill it with life or death, for it is hollow,
Dark wine or bright, fill it, let us go over.

Let me go find my truth, over the river.

WILLIAM SOUTAR [1898–1943]

Destruction

The cities which are falling down
Obey eternal law;
Though steel were adamant, and stone
Confounded by no flaw.

How small the hollow of the hand
And yet within it lie
The walls of Zion, and the sand
Of Nineveh and Troy.

Time is no traitor; and the rage
Of man is not time's child:
The ruination of an age
Grows with the hands that build.

Are not these battlements of war
Cemented on a peace:
And Babel still a leaning tower
Foredoomed by its increase?

ANTONIA WHITE [1899–1980]

Epitaph

By man came death;
Not by my love, my single sun,
Did this seed ripen to its monstrous bloom
But by the moon's unquickening breath
I was undone.

Bury me deep
Lest my love look on me asleep
And see the time-stained face with which I died.
This hasty, swollen mask of yellow wax
Which fear, the clumsy workman botched me up
Blasphemes death's patient marble.
Calmer my living brow,
Purer my cheek that flushes now
With dark decay like rouge.
I wear the face of one who could not stay
For heaven's slow marriage day
That stamps me as death's whore and not his bride.

And from that greedy coupling, hour by hour,
My bastard death grew like an iron flower
Transmuting blood to metal, bone to ice
Between the abhorring thighs.

But my eternal travail is not yet.
Not till this waxen mommet turn to flesh once more
Shall I my true-born death beget.
Not yet, not yet may I put on
Majesty and corruption.

FRANCES BELLERBY [1899–1975]

A Clear Shell

Then fire burned my body to a clear shell.
Though whether the fanning tempest blew from hell
Or heaven I could not, cannot, tell –
Who have no sense
Left for so nice a difference.

But I learned the essential function of extreme pain –
Of liquid fire pouring again and again
And again through the horrified body: such pain
Makes wholly innocent.
Therefore am I impenitent

Today. Today ask no forgiveness,
Having nothing to be forgiven. And my soul, no less
House-proud than at the beginning, shows Death
Smilingly over the place,
Trusting this new face.

CHARLES WREY GARDINER [1901–1981]

Out of the Window

The actual and the spiritual are the flowers of division;
The actual is a cloud seen from a clean window,
The spiritual a window on the merciless rhythm
Of the time scheme of nebulae, the coming
Nearer of the clustered diamonds of desire
Into the focus of seeing until

The spiritual is real
The real the rhythm
Of the dance
Of love.

Where no winds whisper in the reflected image
The trees in the glass are stubborn and unchanged,
The actual fiction is the mind's distemper
The real conundrum of a diffident endeavour,
The fictive clothing of the real with symbols
Of time, my habit and my many
Despairs of precision
Or clouds dispersing
Over the fields
Of the evening.

MADGE HALES [1901–1985]

The Word

What is this that crisps the ear to a bud
Gives light slanting from opaque eyes
And sets the tongue to words?

Stops the thorn print with silver
And shakes dust from the gathering years
Revealing their ultimate gold:

> The serpent that hissed in the wood
> Fled with the browning leaves and is dead
> And the apple blossoms instead.

For the hands with the wounds caught mine
And trapped like sheep in a flood
My sins around me stood.

A sun shook the rocks from my eyes
Clearing a way through the wood of my sight
Till the bough tips stood as cathedrals stand:

The heeding blood on its fleshy way
Knew the precocious veins answered
Knew the hurt in the side flower in blood:

A pale voice heard in a dream set me awake
One voice silenced all others, one word
Fell over me, softer than snow on a hill.

ROY CAMPBELL [1902–1957]

Luís de Camões

Camões, alone, of all the lyric race,
Born in the black aurora of disaster,
Can look a common soldier in the face:
I find a comrade where I sought a master:
For daily, while the stinking crocodiles
Glide from the mangroves on the swampy shore,
He shares my awning on the dhow, he smiles,
And tells me that he lived it all before.
Through fire and shipwreck, pestilence and loss,

Led by the ignis fatuus of duty
To a dog's death – yet of his sorrows king –
He shouldered high his voluntary Cross,
Wrestled his hardships into forms of beauty,
And taught his gorgon destinies to sing.

ADRIAN STOKES [1902–1972]

Kouros Statue

We are the light of honey by the death
        That stings us on.
Trauma seals the withering of champions of love
And irreconciliation quickens loving
Nurtured by the anger of its soils
By airless loams from which to rise.
So for our health death must not die,
So breath, smell, phlegm, tactile sweat
Conspire within the syndrome for this shape
        Figured inert by the stone.

While frames of living crumple,
Each flesh inch saunters in its ill obtuse as gut,
        Kouros statue
Promises procession that shall join
The armatures of health from youth to youth;
That this to life from lifeless stone,
Good images upon the plinth
        Amassed from infant times,
May not be numb, hidden in our horror bed
In misery, pollution and the Camp.

PATRICK MACDONOGH [1902–1961]

Escape to Love: VI

Alone and Godless, stopped by the sudden edge
Of the great quarry slicing the limestone height,
He sees, as from his own life's ultimate ledge,
Symbols of fear and love where slow black families
Creep home from church, home from huge mysteries,
From terrible love home to love's kitchen cares,
New sense of isolation, unawares,
Half-open doors to dim divinities,
To his unwelcome godhead thrust out of sight
By a long indolent act of sacrilege.
He, the unsatisfied, hating the arid light,
Uncharmed, that lit the scrubbed boards of one creed,
Refused the encumbered heritage, loaded with doubt,
Half-envying, half-despising these poor heirs
Enriched by faith. Political orphan, too,
Fouled by his forebears' history he knew
Himself the enemy of that narrow breed,
But no friend to the breed that threw them out.

ROBERT HERRING [1903–1975]

Crystal Palace

In 1851 the world began
To dream about the parliament of man
And built to herald free trade, progress, peace
A structure with a life as short as these,
From whose last ruins in 1936
Rise the first flames of the apocalypse.

JOSEPH MACLEOD ['ADAM DRINAN']
[1903–1984]

The Men of the Rocks: XV

Then anger drew me out of myself like a gun
and I armed myself with a stone to make him dumb
a round hole piercing the white core of the stone

as it was for the seers who studied the trend of things
using such focus to narrow their knowledge in
personal symbol scourging general sins

and as if I too had used the stone as a lens
I saw, troubled and dim, the eyes of my friends
and shadows on faces of ministers and men.

Darkness drew over inevitable as rain
hands groping for picked bones by lamplight faint
but treacherous signals winked in the breasts of the great

as if to steel seals barking along the coast
solidified blobs of oil, slimy and loathsome,
seal with human faces rank-proud, boastful.

A swing of the ground from under faltering feet
a constant pull of the gravity of duty
certainty only in military boots.

Hairy touch of the dark on the back of the hand
Hail of an unknown voice that may be a man's
unchanged the land rolls for them that own the land

Then knowing what was to come was bound to come
I dropped the pebble into the water's gloom
and left the minister and stumbled home.

A small white stone, and a hole piercing the stone,
eye to the socket, brain in brain's control,
as the ancient seers had studied the future, ere they foretold it.

RHODA COGHILL [1903–2000]

from *To His Ghost, Seen After Delirium*

To return from Hades of projected torments,
sorcerer's fancies, devil's fantasies, –
feeling again the high airs of your happiness,
tasting again the wood-sorrel and the clean spring bitterness
of your mysterious shadow-self;
here is a complete recompense;
here a sufficient spiritual gift.

[...]

Since I have fought the pigmy host
that did besiege me so, those wanton thoughts
and not-thoughts, which would steal from me
all memory of being, and at last
steal me from life: – since I have found
again my mind's dear garden, will you not praise me?
will you not give me, victor now,
a crown of olives? – will you not come
bearing a flower from fields of asphodel?

PATRICK KAVANAGH [1904–1967]

Shancoduff

My black hills have never seen the sun rising,
Eternally they look north towards Armagh.
Lot's wife would not be salt if she had been
Incurious as my black hills that are happy
When dawn whitens Glassdrummond chapel.

My hills hoard the bright shillings of March
While the sun searches in every pocket.
They are my Alps and I have climbed the Matterhorn
With a sheaf of hay for three perishing calves
In the field under the Big Forth of Rocksavage.

The sleety winds fondle the rushy beards of Shancoduff
While the cattle-drovers sheltering in the Featherna Bush
Look up and say: 'Who owns them hungry hills
That the water-hen and snipe must have forsaken?
A poet? Then by heavens he must be poor'.
I hear and is my heart not badly shaken?

from *The Great Hunger*

Clay is the word and clay is the flesh
Where the potato gatherers like mechanised scarecrows move
Along the side-fall of the hill – Maguire and his men.
If we watch them an hour is there anything we can prove
Of life as it is broken-backed over the Book
Of Death? Here crows gabble over worms and frogs
And the gulls like old newspapers are blown clear of the
  hedges, luckily.

Is there some light of imagination in these wet clods?
Or why do we stand here shivering?
                                        Which of these men
Loved the light and the queen
Too long virgin? Yesterday was summer. Who was it
   promised marriage to himself
Before apples were hung from the ceilings for Hallowe'en?
We will wait and watch the tragedy to the last curtain,
Till the last soul passively like a bag of wet clay
Rolls down the side of the hill, diverted by the angles
Where the plough missed or a spade stands, straightening
   the way.

[…]

The snipe of Dawn fell like a whirring stone
And Patrick on a headland stood alone.

The pull is on the traces; it is March
And a cold old black wind is blowing from Dundalk.
The twisting sod rolls over on her back –
The virgin screams before the irresistible sock.
No worry on Maguire's mind this day
Except that he forgot to bring his matches.
'Hop back there, Polly, hoy back, woa, wae'.
From every second hill a neighbour watches
With all the sharpened interest of rivalry.
Yet sometimes when the sun comes through a gap
These men know God the Father in a tree:
The Holy Spirit is the rising sap,
And Christ will be the green leaves that will come
At Easter from the sealed and guarded tomb.

[…]

He stands in the doorway of his house
A ragged sculpture of the wind,
October creaks the rotted mattress,
The bedposts fall. No hope. No lust.
The hungry fiend
Screams the apocalypse of clay
In every corner of this land.

On Raglan Road (Air: The Dawning of the Day)

On Raglan Road on an autumn day I met her first and knew
That her dark hair would weave a snare that I might one day rue;
I saw the danger, yet I walked along the enchanted way,
And I said, let grief be a falling leaf at the dawning of the day.

On Grafton Street in November we tripped lightly along the ledge
Of the deep ravine where can be seen the worth of passion's pledge,
The Queen of Hearts still making tarts, and I not making hay –
O I loved too much and by such, by such, is happiness thrown away.

I gave her gifts of the mind, I gave her the secret sign that's known
To the artists who have known the true gods of sound and stone
And word and tint. I did not stint for I gave her poems to say
With her own name there and her own dark hair like clouds over fields
  of May.

On a quiet street where old ghosts meet I see her walking now
Away from me so hurriedly my reason must allow
That I had wooed not as I should a creature made of clay –
When the angel woos the clay he'd lose his wings at the dawn of day.

Epic

I have lived in important places, times
When great events were decided, who owned
That half a rood of rock, a no-man's land
Surrounded by our pitchfork-armed claims.
I heard the Duffys shouting 'Damn your soul'
And old McCabe stripped to the waist, seen
Step the plot defying blue cast-steel –
'Here is the march along these iron stones'.
That was the year of the Munich bother. Which
Was more important? I inclined
To lose my faith in Ballyrush and Gortin
Till Homer's ghost came whispering to my mind.
He said: I made the *Iliad* from such
A local row. Gods make their own importance.

GLYN JONES [1905–1995]

Esyllt Ferch Brychan

As he climbs down our hill, my kestrel rises,
Steering in silence up from empty fields,
A smooth sun brushed brown across his shoulders,
Floating in wide circles, his warm wings stiff.
Their shadows cut; in new soft orange hunting-boots
My lover crashes through the snapping bracken.

The still gorse-hissing hill burns, brags gold broom's
Outcropping quartz; each touched bush spills dew.
Strangely last moment's parting was never sad,
But unreal, like my promised years; less felt
Than this intense white silver snail calligraphy
Scrawled here in the sun between these stones.

Why have I often wanted to cry out
More against his going when he has left my flesh
Only for the night? When he has gone out
Hot from my mother's kitchen, and my combs
Were on the table under the lamp, and the wind
Was banging the doors of the shed in the yard.

Sande

Sande's crucifix, that crisscross star.
The risking saint, naked and upright, scans
His crop of hills and prays against the dark.
The winds pluck off his ripened flesh like leaves,
And then his upright bone-shrub chants, the rigid
Thicket of his skeleton repeats

Its praises from a lip of bone, and through
The lantern holes of both his eyes, his ghost
Erect and vivid, sees his morning star.
The melted lightning yellows round his head;
The vigour of his dropped bones burns the rocks;
Scattered he prays and sees his pulsing star.

Night

This shadow flesh of risen man
Feels on my bones the blurt of pain,
Budges the rock and walks the quays –
The choking bandog snaps his chain.

Her upright body floats the tide,
Fish-teeth pluck her cheek-bones bare;
Naked Mary's candled wave
Blows in the harvest of her hair.

Mark the scandal on the hill
Before our feather-raided sea;
Sway like a bell-tongue, hanging man,
And fret your Judas-fruited tree.

The angelled air, the sea is edged
With fever where black Patmos lies;
Beneath his island aching oak
My thunder-hearted lover dies.

Like grief the rowdy swans return,
Rain has her ear-ring on the thorn;
With broken hands I roll my rock
Back on the Pasc of this raw dawn.

KATHLEEN NOTT [1905–1999]

Taormina

This is the island of never really shade,
But groves where the dull suns the oranges
Made noon at midnight: of the cutting opaque
Black cypresses rearing against the moted mist
Which revolves and smoulders and smokes between ravines
And black tarantulas' arms of lava clawing sea.

An island indeed without chiaroscuro
But glintless surfaces hewn by the light: gesso-
Smudges of peacock on purple abraded sea
Lying as prone and veined as new-won marble:
And all that would seem most fierce and far from home
Held here in a spell which looks like calm of nature:

The island where the dark is all in a well
And they wind it, the dusky people, up the stiff paths
For the dour mules, and over the terraces
Half-hidden in burgeoning: and halt and are tall in an alcove
With the steady burden above their sombre faces,
And turn and vanish beyond the creeping snow of the skyline:

An island almost nothing but lava creeping
And sinking and revolving into the life of the crops:
And therefore no wonder the shadows spurt blue like flames
From the cracks: no wonder the lizards: nor the sulphur mimosa
And grey outcrop of almond blossom: nor, for the people,
The shoved and tilting homes: the lowest most stubborn
Life in the haunts of ruins: and strongpoints made by the graves:
Or falling towards bituminous strata: the rumours

Of caverns and corridors indeterminate under
The pavement of water, booming: or a topless Babel-day.

For the island, the Great Day, belongs to the kingdom of light
And uses the dark for its arts: and there the merciless Sun
Quarries its statues, peoples and ruins: there we,
Sad slaves from the main of darkness bringing our night
Within, wait for probation and release,
As if we could learn in locks to withstand the pressure of light.

LEONARD CLARK [1905–1981]

from *Passage to the Pole*

III

Once, the way through the ice floes to clear water was closed to
me,
Unknown and unsought for,
The bows of my vessel grated aimlessly on with the old stars and
twilight;
There was darkening at sundown, and the crumbling of night
At the first touch of dewfall.
Hill, river and valley, forest and snowfield,
All seen and yet not seen, at hand but not felt,
Heard and not heard,
As they should be with meaning and message.
Till the iceberg and avalanche suddenly thundered and split every
light-point,
Tree, pebble and minute
Into infinity and first death.

IV

Only one frond of one lichen, slender and giving,
Held fast to its surface but went with the movement of all,
And thus was enabled to mock at the chasms of ruins around it.
It knew from dim Eden that birth comes from bleeding,
Water from crystal, and life out of death.
So I saw with new eyes the channel which streamed through the
ice sheet;
But the boat was in doldrums and I was marooned
With the lichen, and could not attempt it.
It was the authentic and definite passage
To lead me with full sails to truth at the pole;
An apocalypse writ in the cleaving of water.

VII

Then spring dropped, an eagle from the peaks of its rangings,
And the winds of the north sang with those of the south
The genesis of an unshackled symphony,
Moving from cadence to cadence to all the four corners
In counterpoint never considered by any composer.
A bird whistled high in the spars and the rigging
And deep in the trees of some passionate orchard
Now flushing to blossom and not with old bleeding;
A flower in slim agony straightened its pale stem
And pitied the ground it had torn with its strivings;
A lamb kicked the womb and parted its mystery
Becoming a shiver of uncertain bleatings
And trembling legs in the teeth of the frost-wind
Racing from hilltop over hedgerow and fold-warmth.
And all sang that new name now shedding its star spray
In blessing upon me.

from *Ultima Thule*

Magnus, we came.
We kept our faith by fiery cross,
Broken cliff and flooded moss,
Magnus, we came,
Not to that high altar where
Sandstone shivers in blue air,
Nor to that dusty, rifled tomb
Where your murdered bones had room,
But to the jagged coast where lay
Weeping ships that destined day
When a sword pierced Egilsay,
Magnus, we came.

Rognvald, we heard
Your poems sung by storm-proud bird,
Echoed by loch and fiord,
Rognvald, we heard
How to Jerusalem you went
Humble of heart, and penitent,
Found forgiveness in each wave
Outdistancing an ocean grave,
And now, each warring bird above
Your roofless church is changed to dove,
And we, pavilioned round with love,
Rognvald, we heard,
Magnus, we came.

N.K. CRUICKSHANK [BORN C 1905]

All Through That Year

All through that year, he, almost still a boy,
Planned, gazed ahead. Time's unsuspected slope
Hooded the sails of gladness and of hope,
As the glass bottle does the full-rigged toy.

This snapshot taken soon before he died –
The smile, the eager look we so well knew –
Perplexes us: we are like children who
Wonder: *How did the tall sails get inside?*

Enemy Action

It has happened before that death came after breakfast
On a scrubbed working day: again and again
Bolts fell, Siloams crumbled, in the past
Upon the young, the usual, the plain.

And the one who simply went across the road
To post a letter or to look around
Holds his redeemed breath, struggles from a load
Of smouldering dread. After, with what profound

Wonder, what thankful, what extensive fears,
Standing alone in the bright summer weather,
Examines that mild choice, which now appears
A least hinge swinging, lightly as it were a feather,
The vast door, opening, of some forty years.

NORMAN CAMERON [1905–1953]

Shepherdess

All day my sheep have mingled with yours. They strayed
Into your valley seeking a change of ground.
Held and bemused with what they and I had found,
Pastures and wonders, heedlessly I delayed.

Now it is late. The tracks leading home are steep,
The stars and landmarks in your country are strange.
How can I take my sheep back over the range?
Shepherdess, show me now where I may sleep.

ETHNA MACCARTHY [1905–1959]

Insomnia

Tell them to go away;
last night Cuchulain slammed the gate five times
and hammered on the window panes,
and then his dog sat on the lawn
and howled and whined,
and after that a beggar banshee keened
and put the Ulster hound to shame.
I have not slept.
Then towards the dawn
strange workmen flickered saffron flags of flame
startling the shadows from their secret raths
to leap and bound about the walls,
and doffed the candle's silken hood,

the wick bereft was blunt and blackened as a clove.
They tapped and tinkered on the frozen pipes,
I heard their creak upon the cistern stairs
till in the peevish light
the clangour of the convent bell
like a ship staggering through clammy fog,
banished all phantoms and I slept.
Tell them to go away till noon
and I will bind in dreams the wraiths
that pilfered last night's sleep.

VERNON WATKINS [1906–1967]

The Collier

When I was born on Amman hill
A dark bird crossed the sun.
Sharp on the floor the shadow fell;
I was the youngest son.

And when I went to the County School
I worked in a shaft of light.
In the wood of the desk I cut my name:
Dai for Dynamite.

The tall black hills my brothers stood;
Their lessons all were done.
From the door of the school when I ran out
They frowned to watch me run.

The slow grey bells they rung a chime
Surly with grief or age.
Clever or clumsy, lad or lout,
All would look for a wage.

I learnt the valley flowers' names
And the rough bark knew my knees.
I brought home trout from the river
And spotted eggs from the trees.

A coloured coat I was given to wear
Where the lights of the rough land shone.
Still jealous of my favour
The tall black hills looked on.

They dipped my coat in the blood of a kid
And they cast me down a pit,
And although I crossed with strangers
There was no way up from it.

Soon as I went from the County School
I worked in a shaft. Said Jim,
'You will get your chain of gold, my lad,
But not for a likely time'.

And one said, 'Jack was not raised up
When the wind blew out the light
Though he interpreted their dreams
And guessed their fears by night'.

And Tom, he shivered his leper's lamp
For the stain that round him grew;
And I heard mouths pray in the after-damp
When the picks would not break through.

They changed words there in the darkness
And still through my head they run,
And white on my limbs is the linen sheet
And gold on my neck the sun.

Portrait of a Friend

He has sent me this
Late and early page
Caught in the emphasis
Of last night's cartonnage,
Crumpled in the post,
Bringing to lamplight
Breath's abatement,
Over- and under-statement,
Mute as a mummy's pamphlet
Long cherished by a ghost.

Who for annunciation has
The white wings of the sheldrake,
Labouring water's praise,
The blind shriek of the mandrake,
Broken shells of story,
Torn earth for love's near head
Raised from time's estuary,
Fed by the raven's bread:
A trespasser in tombs,
He bids the grey dust fall,
Groans in the shaping limbs:
'All stars are in my shawl'.
Who feels the deathbound sighs,
Mocks the Winged Horse's fake,
Toiling, as with closed eyes,

Love's language to remake,
To draw from their dumb wall
The saints to a worldly brothel
That a sinner's tongue may toll
And call the place Bethel.

Trusting a creaking house,
His roof is ruinous,
So mortal. A real wind
Beats on this house of sand
Two tides like ages buffet.
The superhuman, crowned
Saints must enter this drowned
Tide-race of the mind
To guess or understand
The face of this cracked prophet,
Which from its patient pall
I slowly take,
Drop the envelope,
Compel his disturbing shape,
And write these words on a wall
Maybe for a third man's sake.

from *The Ballad of the Mari Lwyd*

Midnight. Midnight. Midnight. Midnight.
Hark at the hands of the clock.
Now dead men rise in the frost of the stars
And fists on the coffins knock.
They dropped in their graves without one sound;
Then they were steady and stiff.
But now they tear through the frost of the ground
As heretic, drunkard and thief.

Why should you fear though they might pass
Ripping the stitch of grief,
The white sheet under the frosted glass,
Crisp and still as a leaf?
Or look through sockets that once were eyes
At the table and white cloth spread?
The terrible, picklock Charities
Raised the erected dead.

Under your walls they gnaw like mice;
Virtue is unmasked.
The hands of the clock betray your vice.
They give what none has asked.
For they have burrowed beneath the graves
And found what the good gave most:
Refuse cast by the righteous waves
In fossil, wraith and ghost.

Chalice and Wafer. Wine and Bread.
And the picklock, picklock, picklock tread.

Midnight. Midnight. Midnight. Midnight.
Hark at the hands of the clock.

Good men gone are evil become
And the men that you nailed down
Clamped in darkness, clamour for rum,
And ravish on beds of down
The vision your light denied them, laid
Above the neglected door;
And the chattering speech of skull and spade
Beckons the banished Poor.

Locked-out lepers with haloes come.
Put out the clock: the clock is dumb.

Midnight. Midnight. Midnight. Midnight.
Hark at the hands of the clock.

The breath of a numb thing, loud and faint:
Something found and lost.
The minute drops in the minute-glass;
Conscience counts the cost.
What mounted, murderous thing goes past
The room of Pentecost?
Sinner and saint, sinner and saint:
A horse's head in the frost.

Midnight. Midnight. Midnight. Midnight.
Hark at the hands of the clock.
What shudders free from the shroud so white
Stretched by the hands of the clock?
What is the sweat that springs in the hair?
Why do the knee-joints knock?
Bones of the night, in the naked air,
Knock, and you hear that knock.

Midnight. Midnight. Midnight. Midnight.
Hark at the hands of the clock.

A knock of the sands on the glass of the grave,
A knock on the sands of the shore,
A knock of the horse's head of the wave,
A beggar's knock on the door.
A knock of a moth on the pane of light,
In the beat of the blood a knock.

Midnight. Midnight. Midnight. Midnight.
Hark at the hands of the clock.

The sands in the glass, the shrinking sands,
And the picklock, picklock, picklock hands.

Midnight. Midnight. Midnight. Midnight.
Hark at the hands of the clock.

The Keen Shy Flame

The keen shy flame holding this poem's ash,
Texture and syllable,
Bears on its point the precious crucible
Transforming utterance to a breath more rash.

Silence is there within the flying bowl
Bright as a waving poppy.
Still from the ignorant pattern falls the copy.
That pivot has all time in its control.

Once through the mummy-cloth it wound its way;
Through music, myrrh and gold
And sacred parchment's wrinkled sounds of mould
Its violet fingers clasped the sleeping clay.

It could not wake the dead lips white and dry
Nor give time's pictures back,
Nor yet release the mute hands gloved in black,
So great a thrall had conquered their last cry.

This in the censer swinging gave forth smoke
And ground the pilgrims' fire;

Silently weeping near the saints' dumb choir
This in the taper gave dark grief a cloak.

Fire-fingers crawling through this last white page
Have played such harps of bone.
Through that black graveyard what faint feet are gone
Where soul puts off the cerements of age.

WILLIAM EMPSON [1906–1984]

Note on Local Flora

There is a tree native in Turkestan,
Or further east towards the Tree of Heaven,
Whose hard cold cones, not being wards to time,
Will leave their mother only for good cause;
Will ripen only in a forest fire;
Wait, to be fathered as was Bacchus once,
Through men's long lives, that image of time's end.
I knew the Phoenix was a vegetable.
So Semele desired her deity
As this in Kew thirsts for the Red Dawn.

Bacchus

The laughing god born of a startling answer
    (Cymbal of clash in the divided glancer
    Forcing from heaven's the force of earth's desire)
Capped a retort to sublime earth by fire
And starred round within man its salt and glitter

(Round goblet, but for star- or whirled-map fitter?
Earth lost in him is still but earth fulfilled),
Troubled the water till the spirit 'stilled
And flowered round tears-of-wine round the dimmed flask
(The roundest ones crack least under this task;
It is the delicate glass stands heat, better than stone.
This is the vessel could have stood alone
Were it not fitted both to earth and sky),
Which trickled to a sea, though wit was dry,
Making a brew thicker than blood, being brine,
Being the mother water which was first made blood,
All living blood, and whatever blood makes wine.

The god arkitect whose coping with the Flood
Groyned the white stallion arches of the main
(And miner deeps that in the dome of the brain
Take Iris' arches' pupillage and Word)
Walked on the bucking water like a bird
And, guard, went round its rampart and its ball
(Columbus' egg sat on earth's garden wall
And held the equitation of his bar;
Waves beat his bounds until he foamed a star
And mapped with fire the skyline that he ploughed),
Trod and divined the inwheeling serene cloud,
(And who knows if Narcissus dumb and bent –)
Shed and fermented to a firmament
(– May use his pool as mirror for the skies?)
Blind Hera's revelation peacock eyes
(Before-and-behind
Trophies the golden throne
May still be planted on;
Incestuous Chaos will breed permanent).
Helled to earth's centre Ixion at the wheel
(He boxed the compassing of his appeal.

Her centaur, born thence, schooled
This hero, the paunched beaker, ether-cooled)
Still makes go round the whirled fooled clouded wheal.

The god who fled down with a standard yard
(Surveying with that reed which was his guard
He showed to John the new Jerusalem.
It was a sugar-cane containing rum,
And hence the fire on which these works depend)
Taught and quivered strung upon the bend
An outmost crystal a recumbent flame
(He drinks all cups the tyrant could acclaim;
He still is dumb, illimitably wined;
Burns still his nose and liver for mankind…)
It is an ether, such an agony.
In the thin choking air of Caucasus
He under operation lies for ever
Smelling the chlorine in the chloroform.
The plains around him flood with the destroyers
Pasturing the stallions in the standing corn.

The herm whose length measured degrees of heat
(Small lar that sunned itself in Mercury
And perked one word there that made space ends meet)
Fluttered his snake too lightly in to see
(Most fertile thief, and journal to inquire)
The mortal Eden forming, and the fire.
A smash resounding in its constancy.
This burst the planet Bacchus in the sky.
Thence dry lone asteroids took heart to be.
So soon the amalgam with mercury
This plumbing: given with it free, the house
Not built with hands: the silver crucible,
Butt-armed: the sovereigns: eats into flaked sloughs.

Paste for the backs of mirrors, there he lies;
Leper scales fall always from his eyes.

She whom the god had snatched into a cloud
Came up my stair and called to me across
The gulf she floated over of despair.
Came roaring up as through triumphal arches
Called I should warm my hands on her gold cope
Called her despair the coping of her fire.

The god in making fire from her despair
Cast from the parabola of falling arches
An arch that cast his focus to the skyline
    Cold focus burning from the other's fire
    Arachne sailing her own rope of cloud
    A Tracer photon with a rocket's life-line
And purged his path with a thin fan of fire

Round steel behind the lights of the god's car

A wheel of fire that span her head across
Borne soaring forward through a crowd of cloud
Robed in fire round as heaven's cope
The god had lit up her despair to fire
Fire behind grates of a part of her despair
And rang like bells the vaults and the dark arches.

ITHELL COLQUHOUN [1906–1988]

The Wax Image

Star of pain
Between cheek and chin
What pin-point is plied from afar?

Star of pain
Between nipple and navel
Whose hatred has sharpened a knife?

Amulet

I went to the Lapithos witch
Who asked me, Are you clean?
Then I will write you the names
Of nine favourable stars
Here in a small packet.
Wear it, wear it always
With a blue bead like an eye
Under the right breast.
This I do; but the left
Still hides a star of pain
Like a mirror cracked, or the bruise
On a pond of frozen water
A break that brings bad luck.

JOHN KNIGHT [1906–1975]

Other Causes of Love: 1

MAELSTROM. I met her once,
the tide running to high,
on a night of light air
and quiet water. Our loves
were elsewhere. She was words of power;
her death always, and already, her own.

Yes, her words neither trickled
into teacups nor thundered or screamed.
They were silent, falling from ocean
to ocean, overwhelming gentleness
of quills of coral, ancient
lodes of ice; they were her death.

She is long alive now and everlasting
as any moment of always, of death,
as this moment going by, being taped.
Her words are love now and everlasting
as any moment of always, of life;
her words alone now, though she is dead.

SHEILA WINGFIELD [1906–1992]

Four Men's Desire

John the Baptist stood with hair
Blown through by the morning air.
Calloused, lean as thorns and brown,
Over the bare land and down
The listening ear of time he spoke
A prologue nothing can revoke.

John, the son of Zebedee,
From the sweet Tiberian sea
With its kingfishers and quail
And oleanders, rips the veil
Of laziness. Through streets the crowd
Argues with him strong and loud.

John, asleep at Ephesus,
Stir your jaws and pray for us!
Faint for love, we tread the ground
As pilgrims on a holy mound,
Waiting to be subtly kissed:
O preacher and Evangelist.

John of Patmos, round your isle
Waves clash and suns beguile
As you mouth, with roughened lips,
A barbarous Apocalypse –
Great visions of a lunatic
Or a world convulsed and sick.

First, the vague prophetic sounds
Usher truth that yet astounds;

Then a contemplative love
Transcends what any deed can prove:
If last, disintegration's fire
Should come, Earth knows four men's desire.

On Looking Down a Street

My mind's disturbed as rooks in the air…
May a thin-shouldered mountain hare
Or shy and meditative donkey,
Cat that gallops down an alley
And the squint-eyed, sandy dab,
Curlew, spider, vole and crab –
Creatures both severe and great
Or nimble as hens running under a gate –
Pray for me now. Lord, how I need
Their cleverness, their careful speed
Or power to be still, their sense,
Their pride and total innocence!
To keep from being fool or wretch
Till some hearse-horses trot this stretch.

VALENTINE ACKLAND [1906–1969]

Poet

As it cries out from under the cover
Of mind, he rises up, leaves his lover,
Leaves his house, wealth, food behind
And goes out.

As it cries to him, he answers, but obeys
Nothing he knows. Intermittently throughout his days
He follows, alone; scared when it shows,
Terrified when it dies to him.

And so on. He trembles when it calls him
But must follow. Suspicious of all that then befalls him,
He loses peace, love, zest and finally life –
And nothing done.

And nothing done. For at the end all he masters
Is the route of the way of numberless disasters,
No more – And where all others have found their grief
He comes, too, to grief – alone.

Dedication Set Over a Crater, 1941

Underneath the paving stones
In a narrow refuge near the city drains,
My young wife in labour brought forth my daughter.

Bombs that screamed down from heaven
Were not portents of divine favour on the birth,
Foretold no noble fortune to the babe;
She lived to cry, to draw breath underground,
To open eyes on darkness and to hear death fall.

Persephone perhaps will weep to see
The mother's shade clasping that shadowy child –
But who will weep for me?

LOUIS MACNEICE [1907–1963]

Prayer Before Birth

I am not yet born; O hear me.
Let not the bloodsucking bat or the rat or the stoat or the
    club-footed ghoul come near me.

I am not born, console me.
I fear that the human race may with tall walls wall me,
    with strong drugs dope me, with wise lies lure me,
        on black racks rack me, in blood-baths roll me.

I am not yet born; provide me
With water to dandle me, grass to grow for me, trees to talk
    to me, sky to sing to me, birds and a white light
        in the back of my mind to guide me.

I am not yet born; forgive me
For the sins that in me the world shall commit, my words
    when they speak me, my thoughts when they think me,
        my treason engendered by traitors beyond me,
            my life when they murder by means of my
                hands, my death when they live me.

I am not yet born; rehearse me
In the parts I must play and the cues I must take when
    old men lecture me, bureaucrats hector me, mountains
        frown at me, lovers laugh at me, the white
            waves call me to folly and the desert calls
                me to doom and the beggar refuses
                    my gift and my children curse me.

I am not yet born; O hear me,
Let not the man who is beast or who thinks he is God
    come near me.

I am not yet born; O fill me
With strength against those who would freeze my
    humanity, would dragoon me into a lethal automaton,
        would make me a cog in a machine, a thing with
            one face, a thing, and against all those
                who would dissipate my entirety, would
                    blow me like thistledown hither and
                        thither or hither and thither
                            like water held in the
                                hands would spill me.

Let them not make me a stone and let them not spill me.
Otherwise kill me.

JOHN HEWITT [1907–1987]

from *The Colony*

I think these natives human, think their code,
though strange to us, and farther from the truth,
only a little so – to be redeemed
if they themselves rise up against the spells
and fears their celibates surround them with.
I find their symbols good, as such, for me,
when I walk in the dark places of the heart;
but name them not to be misunderstood.

I know no vices they monopolise,
if we allow the forms by hunger bred,
the sores of old oppression, the deep skill
in all evasive acts, the swaddled minds,
admit our load of guilt – I mourn the trees
more than as symbol – and would make amends
by fraternising, by small friendly gestures,
hoping by patient words I may convince
my people and this people we are changed
from the raw levies which usurped the land,
if not to kin, to co-inhabitants,
as goat and ox may graze in the same field
and each gain something from proximity;
for we have rights drawn from the soil and sky;
the use, the pace, the patient years of labour,
the rain against the lips, the changing light,
the heavy clay-sucked stride, have altered us;
we would be strangers in the Capitol;
this is our country also, nowhere else;
and we shall not be outcast on the world.

E.J. SCOVELL [1907–1999]

At Night

There is one turning in her bed;
Not her lover come again.
There is one moving in her head;
Not in womb his child, in brain
And body his implanted pain.

She must find out alone a way
To fertilise and bear that thought

That lashes like a child of clay
And leaping sets her body taut,
And yet is dull, and dead, and nought.

Pour her mind's blood over it;
Quicken, knead this lump of pain;
Imagination cover it;
Over stretched stillness let it reign;
Then race and beat it low again.

from *The First Year*

II

Before she first had smiled or looked with calm
Light-answering eyes and claimed to be of man
I put my finger in her shadowy palm,
And her own whispering ones from their chestnut fan
Closed again (as they must) on mine, to a bud.
Then I was where strong currents piled and slackened.
Like a pulse telling all the power of blood
This palm seemed the cavern where alone her darkened
And secret rock-roofed river showed to man
(Except when one inside half-raised the blind
Of her inky eyes, and fierce a dark beam ran
Searchlighting day). So I strayed on her mind;
And thought I trespassed in that covered land.
Her hand seemed private, still an unborn hand.

VII

The days fail: night broods over afternoon:
And at my child's first drink beyond the night
Her skin is silver in the early light.
Sweet the grey morning and the raiders gone.

CHRISTOPHER FRY [1907–2005]

Pain is low against the ground

Pain is low against the ground
And grows like a weed.
Is God still in the air
And in the seed?

Is God still in the air
Now that the sun is down?
They are afraid in the city,
Sleepless in the town,

Cold on the roads,
Desperate by the river.
Can faith for long elude
Prevailing fever?

The world is all with Charon, all, all

The world is all with Charon, all, all,
Even the metal and plume of the rose garden,
And the forest where the sea fumes overhead
In vegetable tides, and particularly
The entrance to the warm baths in Arcite Street
Where we first met; – all! – the sun itself
Trails an evening hand in the sultry river
Far away down by Acheron. I am lonely,
Virilius. Where is the punctual eye
And where is the cautious voice which made
Balance-sheets sound like Homer and Homer sound
Like balance-sheets? The precision of limbs, the amiable
Laugh, the exact festivity? Gone from the world.
You were the peroration of nature, Virilius.
You explained everything to me, even the extremely
Complicated gods. You wrote them down
In seventy columns. Dear curling calligraphy!
Gone from the world, once and for all. And I taught you
In your perceptive moments to appreciate me.
You said I was harmonious, Virilius,
Moulded and harmonious, little matronal
Ox-eye, your package. And then I would walk
Up and down largely, as it were making my own
Sunlight. What a mad blacksmith creation is
Who blows his furnaces until the stars fly upward
And iron Time is hot and politicians glow
And bulbs and roots sizzle into hyacinth
And orchis, and the sand puts out the lion,
Roaring yellow, and oceans bud with porpoises,
Blenny, tunny and the almost unexisting
Blindfish; throats are cut, the masterpiece
Looms out of labour; nations and rebellions

Are spat out to hang on the wind – and all is gone
In one Virilius, wearing his office tunic,
Checking the pence column as he went.
Where's animation now? What is there that stays
To dance? The eye of the one-eyed world is out.

FREDA LAUGHTON [1907–1995]

The Evacuees

There is no sound of guns here, nor echo of guns.
The spasm of bombs has dissolved
Into the determination of the tractor.

Our music now is the rasp of the corncrake
And the wedge-shaped call of the cuckoo
Above leaves tranced in the lap of summer.

We have discovered the grass, curled in the ditches.
We have combed it with rakes in the hayfields,
And coiffed it in lion-coloured stacks.

We have stroked milk, warm and gentle from the cow,
The placid primitive milk, before bottles
Sterilise its mild wonder.

We have met the bland smile of eggs in the willow-basket;
Returned the stolid stare of cheeses ripening on the shelf;
Warmed ourselves at the smell of baking bread.

We have seen food, the sacrament of life,
Not emasculate and defunct upon dishes, but alive,
Springing from the earth after the discipline of the plough.

DENIS DEVLIN [1908–1959]

Lough Derg

The poor in spirit on their rosary rounds,
The jobbers with their whiskey-angered eyes,
The pink bank clerks, the tip-hat papal counts,
And drab, kind women their tonsured mockery tries,
Glad invalids on penitential feet
Walk the Lord's majesty like their village street.

With mullioned Europe shattered, this Northwest,
Rude-sainted isle would pray it whole again:
(Peasant Apollo! Troy is worn to rest.)
Europe that humanised the sacred bane
Of God's chance who yet laughed in his mind
And balanced thief and saint: were they this kind?

Low rocks, a few weasels, lake
Like a field of burnt gorse; the rooks caw;
Ours, passive, for man's gradual wisdom take
Firefly instinct dreamed out into law;
The prophets' jewelled kingdom down at heel
Fires no Augustine here. Inert, they kneel;

All is simple and symbol in their world,
The incomprehended rendered fabulous.
Sin teases life whose natural fruits withheld
Sour the deprived nor bloom for timely loss:
Clan Jansen! less what magnanimity leavens
Man's wept-out, fitful, magniloquent heavens

Where prayer was praise, O Lord! the Temple trumpets
Cascaded down Thy sunny pavilions of air,
The scroll-tongued priests, the galvanic strumpets,
All clash and stridency gloomed upon Thy stair;
The pharisees, the exalted boy their power
Sensually psalmed in Thee, their coming hour!

And to the sun, earth turned her flower of sex,
Acanthus in the architects' limpid angles;
Close priests allegorised the Orphic egg's
Brood, and from the Academy, tolerant wranglers
Could hear the contemplatives of the Tragic Choir
Drain off man's sanguine, pastoral death-desire.

It was said stone dreams and animal sleeps and man
Is awake; but sleep with its drama on us bred
Animal articulate, only somnambulist can
Conscience like Cawdor give the blood its head
For the dim moors to reign through druids again.
O first geometer! tangent-feelered brain

Clearing by inches the encircled eyes,
Bolder than the peasant tiger whose autumn beauty
Sags in the expletive kill, or the sacrifice
Of dearth puffed positive in the stance of duty
With which these pilgrims would propitiate
Their fears; no leafy, medieval state

Of paschal cathedrals backed on earthy hooves
Against the craftsmen's primary-coloured skies
Whose gold was Gabriel on the patient roofs,
The parabled windows taught the dead to rise,
And Christ the Centaur, in two natures whole,
With fable and proverb joinered body and soul.

Water withers from the oars. The pilgrims blacken
Out of the boats to masticate their sin
Where Dante smelled among the stones and bracken
The door to Hell (O harder Hell where pain
Is earthed, a casuist sanctuary of guilt!).
Spirit bureaucracy on a bet built

Part by this race when monks in convents of coracles
For the Merovingian centuries left their land,
Belled, fragrant; and honest in their oracles
Bespoke the grace to give without demand,
Martyrs Heaven winged nor tempted with reward.
And not ours, doughed in dogma, who never have dared

Will with surrogate palm distribute hope:
No better nor worse than I who, in my books,
Have angered at the stake with Bruno and, by the rope
Watt Tyler swung from, leagued with shifty looks
To fuse the next rebellion with the desperate
Serfs in the sane need to eat and get;

Have praised, on its thunderous canvas, the Florentine smile
As man took to wearing his death, his own,
Sapped crisis through cathedral branches (while
Flesh groped loud round dissenting skeleton)
In soul, reborn as body's appetite:
Now languisht back in body's amber light,

Now is consumed. O earthly paradise!
Hell is to know our natural empire used
Wrong, by mind's moulting, brute divinities.
The vanishing tiger's saved, his blood transfused.
Kent is for Jutes again and Glasgow town
Burns high enough to screen the stars and moon.

Well may they cry who have been robbed, their wasting
Shares in justice legally lowered until
Man his own actor, matrix, mould and casting,
Or man, God's image, sees his idol spill.
Say it was pride that did it, or virtue's brief:
To them that suffer it is no relief.

All indiscriminate, man, stone, animal
Are woken up in nightmare. What John the Blind
From Patmos saw works and we speak it. Not all
The men of God nor the priests of mankind
Can mend or explain the good and broke, not one
Generous with love prove communion;

Behind the eyes the winged ascension flags,
For want of spirit by the market blurbed,
And if hands touch, such fraternity sags
Frightened this side the dykes of death disturbed
Like Aran Islands' bibulous, unclean seas:
Pietà: but the limbs ache; it is not peace.

Then to see less, look little, let hearts' hunger
Feed on water and berries. The pilgrims sing:
Life will fare well from elder to younger,
Though courage fail in a world-end, rosary ring.
Courage kills its practioners and we live,
Nothing forgotten, nothing to forgive,

We pray to ourself. The metal moon, unspent
Virgin eternity sleeping in the mind,
Excites the form of prayer without content;
Whitethorn lightens, delicate and blind,
The negro mountain, and so, knelt on her sod,
This woman beside me murmuring *My God! My God!*

SILVIA DOBSON [1908–1994]

Prophecy

Peace, when it comes
will silt the bloody rivers
with sand of clotted quiddity, with shale of scorn.

Torn threads of feeling
must go graft themselves on granite rock,
on snarling cactus trees.

Till reason is a desert and we lead
a child without anguish
to divine wells.

Threshold

I am no longer inconsequent
for I have found comfort
in my own skill and dexterity,
my own wisdom.

Wrapped in warmth,
I shall not feel cold again;
never starve, never die of thirst,
never throw myself down.

– Youth went out with the whirlwind
to drown himself in a deep pool. –

But I am locked in life
and cannot escape.

HUBERT NICHOLSON [1908–1996]

War Factory

In this imprisoned congo berserk suns
rise with the furnace-doors, make random morn,
set on the molten wave that tideless runs
and from the heat our birds of ice are born.
Here we the oil-black slaves have mastery
creators of the fire and the force
who weave their nests of water and set free
metallic snowbirds, auk and albatross.
Bridled and bitted angels caught in hell,
the endless line of ingots turns and swings
dipping and tossing as our chains compel
till lathe and hammer blow release their wings.
And through cell-windows small we see them fly
The lucid life-and-death way of the sky.

KATHLEEN RAINE [1908–2003]

Invocation

There is a poem on the way,
there is a poem all round me,
the poem is in the future,
the poem is in the upper air
above the foggy atmosphere
it hovers, a spirit
that I would make incarnate.
Let my body sweat
let snakes torment my breast
my eyes be blind, ears deaf, hands distraught
mouth parched, uterus cut out,
belly slashed, back lashed,
tongue slivered into thongs of leather
rain stones inserted in my breasts,
head severed,

if only the lips may speak,
if only the god will come.

ROBERT GARIOCH [1909–1987]

During a Music Festival

Cantie in seaside simmer on the dunes,
I fling awa my dowp of cigarette
whaur bairns hae biggit castles out of sand
and watch the reik rise frae the parapet.

Suddenlike I am back in Libya;
yon's the escarpment, and a bleizan plane,
the wee white speck that feeds the luift wi reik,
dirkins a horror-pictur on my brain.

And aye the reik bleeds frae the warld's rim
as it has duin frae Babylon and Troy,
London, Bonn, Edinbro, time eftir time.
And great Beethoven sang a Hymn to Joy.

JAMES REEVES [1909–1978]

To Norman Cameron 1905–1953

I asked the river-god a song
With which to mourn your fallen head.
No answer: but a low wind crept
About the stones of his dry bed.

The fingers of insomnia
Turning the pages of self-hate
Are like the incurious wind that stirred
The papery reeds on that estate.

In other days I knew the god
Who flashed and chuckled in the sun.
Where has he taken now his moods
Of shadow and his sense of fun?

The requiem I might have had
From him you would have understood:
Just as you also understood
How hard a thing it is, though good,

To hold your tongue and wait your time
When there is nothing to be said.
I know it now: I knew you both
But he is gone, and you are dead.

Even the wind has stopped; no sound
In this dull air is born to live;
So I my desperate silences
To you my friend and poet give.

BERNARD SPENCER [1909–1963]

Out of Sleep

Surfacing out of sleep she feared
voices in the sky talking
with thick tongues. Night flashed
brightening her eyelids. Yet as panic cleared
she knew those voices never spoke the harsh
brogue of the guns. And then the rain
sighed in the leaves; it was thunder.
The rain said, hush.

It has been peace in our world a year:
what worse-than-memories seep
to infect our nights with fear
up from the angers of that other war,
ours copy here?
What towns burn on what darker coast of sleep,
how many histories deep?

LYNETTE ROBERTS [1909–1995]

Poem from Llanybri

If you come my way that is…
Between now and then, I will offer you
A fist full of rock cress fresh from the bank
The valley tips of garlic red with dew
Cooler than shallots, a breath you can swank

In the village when you come. At noon-day
I will offer you a choice bowl of cawl
Served with a 'lover's' spoon and a chopped spray
Of leeks or savori fach, not used now,

In the old way you'll understand. The din
Of children singing through the eyelet sheds
Ringing smith hoops, chasing the butt of hens;
Or I can offer you Cwmcelyn spread

With quartz stones from the wild scratchings of men:
You will have to go carefully with clogs
Or thick shoes for it's treacherous the fen,
The East and West Marshes also have bogs.

Then I'll do the lights, fill the lamp with oil,
Get coal from the shed, water from the well;
Pluck and draw pigeon with crop of green foil
This your good supper from the lime-tree fell.

A sit by the hearth with blue flames rising,
No talk. Just a stare at 'Time' gathering
Healed thoughts, pool insight, like swan sailing
Peace and sound around the home, offering

You a night's rest and my day's energy.
You must come – start this pilgrimage
Can you come? – send an ode or elegy
In the old way and raise our heritage.

The New Perception of Colour

And I shall take as my Example the Raid on Swansea

I, that is Xebo7011 pass out into the chill-blue-air and join Xebn559162 her sack apron greening by the light of the moon. I read around her hips: 'BEST CWT: CLARK'S COW-CAKES, H.T.5.' I do not laugh because I love my peasant friend. The night is clear, spacious, a himmel blue, and the stars minute pinpricks. The elbow-drone of jerries burden the sky and our sailing planes tack in and out with their fine metallic hum.

Oh! look how lovely she is caught in those lights! Oh!

From our high village on the Towy we can see straight down the South Wales Coast. Every searchlight goes up, a glade of magnesium waning to a distant hill which we know to be Swansea.

Swansea's sure to be bad; look at those flares like a swarm of orange bees.

They fade and others return. A collyrium sky, chemically washed CuDH2. A blasting flash impels Swansea to riot! higher, absurdly higher, the sulphuric clouds roll with their stench of ore, we breathe naphthalene air, the pillars of smoke writhe and the astringent sky lies pale at her sides. A Jerry overhead drops two flares; the cows returning to their sheds wear hides of cyanite blue, their eyes GLINTING OPALS! We, alarmed, stand puce beneath another flare, our blood distilled, cylindricals of glass. The raiders scatter, then return and form a piratic ring within our shores. High explosives splash up blue, white, and green. We know all copper compounds are poisonous, we know also where they are.

Bleached, Rosie turns to fetch in the cows. I lonely, return to my hearth, there is a quiet clayfire with blue flames rising that would bring solace to any heart.

Lamentation

To the village of lace and stone
Came strangers. I was one of these
Always observant and slightly obscure.
I roamed the hills of bird and bone
Rescuing bees from under the storm:
Five hills rocked and four homes fell
The day I remember the raid so well.
Eyes shone like cups chipped and stiff
The living bled the dead lay in their grief
Cows, sheep, horses, all had got struck
Black as bird wounds, red as wild duck.

Dead as icebone breaking the hedge.
Dead as soil failing of good heart.

Dead as trees quivering with shock
At the hot death from the plane.

O the cold loss of cattle
With their lovely big eyes.
The emptiness of sheds,
The rick stacked high.
The breast of the hills
Will soon turn grey
As the dogs that grieve
And I that fetched them in:
For the good gates are closed
In the yard down our way.

'But my loss. My loss is deeper
Than Rosie's of Chapel House Farm
For I met death before birth:
Fought for life and in reply lost
My own with a cold despair.
I hugged the fire around the hearth
To warm the beat and wing
Yet knew the symbol when it came
Lawrence had found the same.
I threw the starling hard as stone
Into the breaking earth…'

Dead as icebone breaking the hedge.
Dead as soil failing of good heart.
Dead as trees quivering with shock
At the hot death from the plane.

O the salt loss of life
Her lovely green ways.
The emptiness of crib

And big stare of night.
The breast of the hills
Yield a bucket of milk:
But the crane no longer cries
With the round birds at dawn
For the home has been shadowed
A storm of sorrow drowned the way.

The Shadow Remains

To speak of everyday things with ease
And arrest the mind to a simpler world
Where living tables are stripped of a cloth;

Of wood on which I washed, sat at peace:
Cooked duck, shot on an evening in peacock cold:
Studied awhile: wrote: baked bread for us both.

But here by the hearth with leisured grace
I prefer to speak of the vulgar clock that drips
With the falling of rain: woodbine tips, and yarrow

Spills, lamp, packet of salt, and twopence of mace
That sit on the shelf edged with a metal strip,
And below, brazier fire that burns our sorrow,

Dries weeping socks above on the rack: that knew
Two angels pinned to the wall – again two.

from *Gods with Stainless Ears*

from PART I

Today the same tide leans back, blue rinsing bay,
With new beaks scissoring the air, a care-away
Cadence of sight and sound, poets and men
Rediscovering them. Saline mud
Siltering, wet with marshpinks, fresh as lime stud

Whitening fields, gulls and stones attending them;
Curlews disputing coverts pipe back: stem
Plaintive legs deep in the ironing edge, that
Outshines the shale, a railway line washed flat,
Or tin splintered from a crab-green cave.

This is Saint Cadoc's Day. All this Saint Cadoc's
Estuary: and that bell tolling, Abbey paddock.
Sunk. – Sad as ancient monument of stone.
Trees vail, exhale cyprine shade, widowing
Homeric hills, green pinnacles of bone.

Escaping from these, tomb and cave, quagmires
Migrate; draw victim eyes with lustre sheen, suck
Confervoid residue from gillette veins: who talk
Now yield, calling others, those who walk
From Llanstephan, Llangain, and Llanybri.

No watereyes squinting or too near madness
Could fail such a trek. In this same old soddenness
In deep corridor graves culverts open; their
Gates kedged in mud, preening feathered air
Elucidating shapes flecked with woolglints

And small affiliated tares. – So walk swiftly by,
For today, *pridian*, tears ravens wings to grate
The bay, and John Roberts covered with ligustrum,
Always sanitary and discreet, rows to and fro from
Bell house to fennel, floating quietly on the tide.

from PART II

We must uprise O my people. Though
Secretly trenched in sorrel, we must
Upshine, outshine the day's sun. And day
Intensified by the falling haggard
Of rain shall curve our smile with straw.

Bring plimsole plover to the tensile sand
And with cuprite crest and petulant feet
Distil our notes into febrile weeds
Crisply starched at the water-rail of tides:
On gault and green stone a gramophone stands,

In zebeline stripes strike out the pilotless
Age: from saxophone towns brass out the dead:
Disinter futility that we entombing men
Might curb our runaway hearts. –
On tamarisk; on seafield pools shivering

With water-cats, ring out the square slate notes
Shape the birdbox trees with neumes, wind sound
Singular into cool and simple corners
Round pale bittern grass and all unseen
Unknown places of sheltered rubble

Where whimbrels, redshanks, sandpipers ripple
For the wing of living. Under tin of earth,
From wooden boles where owls break music;
From this killing world against humanity
Uprise against, – outshine the day's sun.

Corymb of coriander: each ray frosted
Incandescent: by square stem held, hispid,
And purple spotted. Twice pinnate with fronds
Of chrome. Laid higher than the exulted hedge;
By pure collated disc of daisy glittering

White on a red powdered stem. By cusp of leaves
Held low to ground; this coriander cane,
Colonnade of angelica, chervil, fennel,
Parsley, aniseed, caraway, yarrow,
All kitchen's frescade culled and tied away.

SEÁN RAFFERTY [1909–1993]

The old stag crew before the light

The old stag crew before the light
and there and near it sang amends
for dwindled ash and candle ends
and for the page that looked as though
a bird had grounded on the white
the pure impediment of snow.

The ash ends the draughts that mouse
over the floor, the adding clock,
tick and half tick, owl's chimney talk,

rats' honeymoons, I thought I knew
the hour's small noises through the house:
and suddenly the old stag crew.

What early light had edged his comb?
He clapped his wings and made time fly
like dust from feathers and his cry
went raftering back till it was heard
beyond the straw built rooves of Rome;
o dawn bright sill o gilded bird.

Aristodemus wakened up
cradled in cramp, a mouth like plush,
eyes stuck in glue and tried to push
the night away and belched and through
the rift he made he saw the cup
and it was then the old stag crew.

A far cry on a favouring wind:
the great cup passed from left to right:
what star have I outwatched tonight
I sit no longer time's dull child.
But I have sat to supper's end
and heard the muses reconciled.

He counted up his ha'pence

He counted up his ha'pence
the golden silence broke;
He said I was an acorn once
I might have been an oak;
the first to go are livelier
than those who last too long.

I lived to be a proverb
I might have died a song.

It was a folly of my grief

It was a folly of my grief
that broke the branch and set it there
in heavy splendour, flower and leaf
bowed to the midnight air.
And still no footstep on the stair.
I thought that if a ghost should come
the scent of flowers will guide her home.

Last spring from that same tree she brought
the smouldering lilac wet with rain
and set it where it stands, the thought
is all my thought; and pain.
She brought and will not bring again.
And for that thought and pain I kept
the tears my childhood never wept.

How short a time since war and death
mourned at our marriage. She is dead.
Go stumble in the streets beneath
the flags that will not lift your head
into their peace and hush unsaid
under the cheering crowds your cry
that they should live and she should die.

You grow like a beanstalk

You grow like a beanstalk
as tall as a tale;
twining your time a garland, the leaves are all
shaped in a single heart, to climb until
you stand as high as your wish and what's over the wall
flowers in your eye, a marvel, to teach the tongue
the scale of tomorrow and elsewhere. The song to be sung.

Once, o legends ago,
in the halfway house
by the fire where bedward candles beg their flame
I read you the tale of the thumb-tall girl who was swept
away on a lily leaf, the toad, the mouse;
you so still on my lap I thought you slept.
But the story darkened. The mole's long galleries came
nowhere to guess or glimmer of ending; grief.
Tears that would not, would not be comforted, no
though the risen bird was king and south was home
would not: away on a woman's tears far past belief
in a happy ever and after I watched you go
Ceres in search of her child a child gone down to the dark.
I heard you a woman cry
and born a maiden you wept for the maidens who die.

Soon I listen
and you, the traveller, make
plans for an early start; your turn to tell
the other side of the story. The path you take
is worn like a wish: beasts are clumsy and kind
the birds are concerned about orphans, nothing has changed, the lake
copies its own landscape of turrets and trees, you find
the house they told you was ruined and there at last

the sun is taking the girl in her bridal dress,
the six white horses are waiting, across the park
bells are rising, immaculate doves fly past
over your future and after them into the dark
my fears go up like fireworks, salute and bless
as far as a wish can see or a heart can guess.

The candles yawning and the fire gone out

The candles yawning and the fire gone out.
Silence, your sin; let silence make amends.
You will not write a line and if you wrote
what would you write but epitaphs and ends?

RANDALL SWINGLER [1909–1967]

Lazarus or The Walking Dead: 1

On the hither bank of battle
He made a deal with Death, to take away
The aching pack of Fear; should he gainsay
All hope, all expectation, all regret.
Death signed, and kept his pledge.
The Soldier laughed and sang in the sweat of hell,
And by sheer accident defaulted on his debt,
Emerged bewildered on life's further edge.
Haunted, returning to the source of hate,
He kicks the dust of ruin which he made
But finds no key; and is not justified.
He owes a debt to death and has not paid.

How will he ever expiate
The guilt of being alive?

JOHN PUDNEY [1909–1977]

Envoi: Twelfth Night

Come, holly, burn.
Let January with a pallid oil
Of light, yellow, above iron frontiers discern
Our hope, the crocus pointed under soil.

Go, holly leaf
Of festivals and memories of friends:
Go garlanded with fire. Now let regrets and grief
With dawn suspire. Now means seek ends.

NESSIE DUNSMUIR [1909–1999]

Poem

I would have chosen children,
the breathing hearth. And made my own
ritual in winter, birth and bone.
Not this wordy ferment in the fingers,
this sailing hunger capsized in the breast.
I would have chosen children,
and roofed with rose of fire their early east.

Acorn Mile Miracle Tree

I am that acorn, mile, miracle, tree
reared bright, and broken on love's own wheel;
for from the first constructed anarchy
of mountains seeded in early earthquakes of air
or gravity calling all falling wonders home,
nothing not me was floated on the first waters.

In my blood's roadway steps the white alp.
My breath is halted by origin's ape cry.
Snowfields are falling and though my quick hand
ungrudging lift the fledgling from the pool,
housed in the halls and lulls hurling my heart
sleeps the tornado and the volcano's violence.

My love already lives in tomorrow's flowering
and summers all the wind with bees and rivers.
Because my eyes have cooled the sky's far springs
no water waves but wears my eyelid's ease.
The sun goes down his golden length to lie
warm in my bone and in the warm earth's deep.
The night breaks in my heart. The berries gather
in a standing wheel of stars. The bright locks keep.

For a Winter Lover

I should have been more scrupulous
of that first hour.
More measured against future loss
the live and lovely hazard where
soul signalled soul
through body's tenderness.

But what had loss to do with us
held there and holding all
the blinding universe?

Stranger in my arms
man clown and angel
bearing like flowers
the everlasting annunciation.

I do not know and never shall
what grave or joyful mystery
inhabits your head's holiness,
but my strong heart has made your ease,
my eyes inherit a lightstruck world.

MALCOLM LOWRY [1909–1957]

Success is like some horrible disaster

Success is like some horrible disaster
Worse than your house burning, the sounds of ruination
As the roof tree falls succeeding each other faster
While you stand, the helpless witness of your damnation.

Fame like a drunkard consumes the house of the soul
Exposing that you have worked for only this –
Ah, that I had never known such a treacherous kiss
And had been left in darkness forever to work and fail.

Kingfishers in British Columbia

A mad kingfisher
Rocketing about in the
Red fog at sunrise

Now sits
On the alder
Post that tethers the floats
Angrily awaiting his mate.
Here she

Comes, like a left wing
Threequarter cutting through toward
The goal in sun-lamped
Fog at Rosslyn Park at half
Past three in halcyon days.

STEPHEN SPENDER [1909–1995]

from *Study for First Ode: Destruction and Resurrection*

Driven under nightmare
Of a disrupting star: exiled into dreams,
Spirit and flesh of nature:
Being, fury-pursued, haunted
By throbbing net of high advancing steel
Wings: dive with me where
Beneath the ascendant doom which seems
Destructive in each downwards-pointing feature
By human will invented,
In your uttermost need, my words may feel

Your agony, England!
Arise, rose of the blood,
Blaze from thorns of the heart:
Martyred blood of garlanded past days
Burn from the bombed and bitter island:
May your flesh petals torn to dust apart
By the blast of rays,
In burning beauty revive their flushed transparent good!

Covered with ashes is your statued past,
Once sunlit, where each soul his heritage
From birth-to-death-span tilled, plotting deliberate choice
Of his willed good or evil flowers.
Destiny more glittering and vast
Than simple single sight fading through life to growing death
and knowledge,
Blinds faith's towers.
Nor is there any voice,

Nor any bell to mourn the loss
Of that which died before
– The faith the stones are shaped to imitate,
Without whose fire beneath
Aspiring to the Climax of the Cross,
The lion of rage is loosed to roar,
The once-caged Satan to create
The death of life, and then this life of death!

Apocalyptic fury,
Blaze, blaze, flower of these black skies!
Burst open with vermilion the packed night
Of money, in the silent city!
With tongues of glory
Of blood, wring eyesight

From the puked lids of long unseeing eyes!
Grind the hearts that ground no bread of pity

Into pity's opposite
Where stones melt, steel burns, mind
Vomits entrails, love sees hate
Dancing a star of triumph. Let virtue paint a devil
Riding over the ruins in a rite:
That life, by man-made powers denied, may find
A song released by the rejoicing fate
Of world-devouring evil.

Crack doom, crow cock,
Saw with your shrill combed shriek the roofs!
Tomorrow, down with jagged lightning! Chariot
Of thunder, shake the drum of night!
Sword, split the temple's pedestal of rock!
Coursers, draw on with your avenging hooves
The sullen barbarian marauder and his followers, to divide by lot
Crucified light.

W.R. RODGERS [1909–1969]

from *Epilogue*

I am Ulster, my people an abrupt people
Who like the spiky consonants in speech
And think the soft ones cissy; who dig
The *k* and *t* in orchestra, detect sin
In sinfonia, get a kick out of
Tin cans, fricatives, fornication, staccato talk,
Anything that gives or takes attack,
Like Micks, Tagues, tinkers' gets, Vatican.
An angular people, brusque and Protestant,
For whom the word is still a fighting word,
Who bristle into reticence at the sound
Of the round gift of the gab in Southern mouths.
Mine were not born with silver spoons in gob,
Nor would they thank you for the gift of tongues;
The dry riposte, the bitter repartee's
The Northman's bite and portion, his deep sup
Is silence; though, still within his shell,
He holds the old sea-roar and surge
Of rhetoric and Holy Writ.
Three hundred years ago our foundling fathers
With farthing fists and thistles in their eyes
Were planted on this foreshore,
Bibles for bibs and bloody pikes for rattles
And tombs for keeps. There was not time
To wade through wedding to a birth.
Calvin and culverin sang the cradle-song
And Cromwell made the bed.
Put to a frugal breast of swollen hopes
They did their levelling best and left it flat
As water. Winding-sheet and swaddling-band

Were one. Needle-flute and thimble-drum
Stitched the way to kingdom-come, to Derry,
Aughrim, Enniskillen, and the Boyne:
Rat-a-ta-ta, rat-a-ta-ta, rat-a-ta-ta,
Humdrummery of history.
And I, born to the purple passage,
Was heir to all that Adamnation
And hand-me-down of doom, the late comer
To the worn-out womb.
The apple blushed for me below Bellevue,
Lagan was my Jordan, Connswater
My washpot, and over Belfast
I cast out my shoe.

NORMAN MACCAIG [1910–1996]

You enter one by one

You enter one by one
for my most burglar-proof
and guarded thoughts begin
to welcome in this thief

and can feel it no crime
to manacle themselves
inside their shuttered room,
tying their wrists with curves

of their own thoughts. Thought
tells lying thought to watch,
restless with its delight
to hear the stirring latch

as one by one you come
changing the shadow curves
in every littered room
with all your shining selves.

The rusty wind wrestles on the quay

The rusty wind wrestles on the quay
where I romantically drive my dogs of darkness.
What is the power in men that makes an ocean of brine
out of a tear, out of a tear's impulse, out of what
should bring a tear into another's eyes?
From the light that breeds in the overhead sky

one vision, transmitted in nerves
and distilled in the talking vault of a skull,
is used to crowd the air with private harpies
archangels angels cherubims Gabriels.
A mood's moment chirping in the hairy shell
of a sickened ear fills the sky's waves

with the piercing universal trumpet,
the golden tongue braying of guilt and blood
or the fanfare usher of an immaculate messiah.
I mince about the slippery stones of my harbour
retrieving the wrack and jetsam of a stranded world
from the half inch between a cockle and a limpet,

watch my day die in a fire of revolution,
night like the middle ages snuff out the sky,
ripple like chaos sigh out on a pebble
myself. Myself stuck like a stick insect
on the peeled stem of the world, humourless and grey
on the colourless collapse of nation upon nation.

Answering the dry dust and the green-shaded lamp

Answering the dry dust and the green-shaded lamp
the darkness bundled under desks and in corners,
law leaps out cackling with seventy years,
death's threshold jerking from its limber ankles;
and wisdom like its own pages soiled and limp
sings with a senile bravura and idly twinkles

a pencil spot of light on the crushing pyramid
which forged in sand to hide the dead from sand
rears a monument vivid to the blind.
The fence we fumble with, seeking to discover
lands beyond ours and with them identical burned
in fire before the Israelites. They saw it clamber

in mushroom clouds over the icy desert.
It was a star voyaging to Bethlehem.
It crowed three times. It is the end of dream,
and on this side of dream we arm it with sleep,
prickle it with dead codes and the delirium of art
and haunt it with ourselves, the ghosts of hope.

The Golden Branch

Sometimes to lose myself in brooches and bangles
of small words found in the walking of a dream,
to loose crinkling salvoes against the mute wave
that heaves heaven in a wilderness, to come home
glad with a common butterfly as spoils of the jungles
deep on these ordinary fields, content my love
of fathoming the darkness of the dangerous grove.

Nerveless desire laughs in the sprinkled sun
and soothes its weariness with a shadow's edge.
What monstrous birth would be in me, what end
would round this trifling dream if I could lodge
one thought in that wild darkness? For I might then
see hell's mouth opening, and find in my hand
the golden branch and murder on my head.

Stone Pillow

The malediction that each moment is
Falls from your lips – or what I dream is there.
I fight with an angel, and a Jacob stair
Shuts me from heaven with heavenly distances.
Why should such dreams mock me? – that mock you, too,
          As any dream must do.

I need create no windy plain where gods
Might seem to insinuate themselves in what
Is matter for human lust and human thought
(My head to lie, a clod between two clods,
No doubt, while heroes briskly make a myth
          To immortalise you with).

For all the Helens made golden by a word
Are your projection on the marvellous screen,
A different wonder, the always might-have-been.
You're the dull fact, the mortally absurd
That gives sense to all Troys and makes them fall
          Into the possible.

Immortal ordinariness – is that
A meaning you can have? Cuchulain, changed
Extraordinarily, but still Cuchulain, ranged
Tall ranks of enemies and laid them flat.
The battle done, he became like other men.
    – Cuchulain once again?

Outward and inward equally in you
Display the other. Let no crisis be,
To loose you in depredation upon me;
How could I bear to be destroyed and through
My falling forces see you pass, no more
    Immortal than before?

My dreams are angel-like because their praise
Fills the distance between us, measuring
A space and time with what they are. You'll bring
Their heavenly ladder down when I can raise
My human head from this stone pillow and stare
    At you and the desert there.

ALAN ROOK [1910–1990]

Dunkirk Pier

Deeply across the waves of our darkness fear
like the silent octopus feeling, groping, clear
as a star's reflection, nervous and cold as a bird,
tells us that pain, tells us that death is near.

Why should a woman telling above her fire
incantations of evening, thoughts that are
older and paler than history, why should this lark
exploring extinction and oneness of self and air

remind us that, lonely and lost as flowers in deserted
weed-mastered gardens, each faint face averted
from the inescapable confusion, for each of us slowly
death on his last, most hideous journey has started?

What was our sin? – that heartless to the end
falls now the heavy sickle on foe, on friend,
and those that we love, value and regret
surrender quickest to death's empty hand.

Failure to suffer? We who in years past
have suffered, yes, in this or that, but in the last
irrevocable act of suffering, as a dog suffers deeply,
blindly, completely, are not versed.

What hope for the future? Can we who see the tide
ebbing along the shore, the greedy, lined
with shadows, dare with puny words support
a future which belongs to others? Dare we bind

now, at this last moment of sunshine above
the crests of oncoming events, like waves which move
remorselessly nearer, future generations
with sacrifice? We who taught hate, expect them to love?

NOËL WELCH [C 1911–2017]

The Red Shirt

I liked your red shirt, it was really more rusty
than red, as if you had rolled in the earth
or wrapped yourself in the remnant of a sail.
A tall barbaric age rose behind you,
from a distance you looked flayed,
close I could count your ribs.
I first saw you on the quay unravelling a rope;
you have a knack of reducing things
to their simplest form. I like simplicity.
Before a redeeming act one needs time;
loose ends must be knotted, sleeves rolled up.
Once you helped me set the lobster pots
but when it was time to harvest the catch
I found you spreadeagled on a promontory.
Beside you held by four white stones that bloody shirt,
it claimed allegiance, spread revolt.
At eight o'clock propped against my door,
you were more piratical than the setting sun.
Last summer I scraped the barrel to provide
for two.

This summer you have a new shirt.
Be off. Salvation is not now, nor tomorrow.
I have fish to clean, nets to mend.

Lazarus

Originally, you would not have crossed
The road to talk to him. Why seek him now?

The distinct is clear. I need clarity
The unobstructed, the evident, the free.

A part of life again who was a part
Of the dark: he is as indistinct as you.

Today is not yesterday, tomorrow neither;
I am not what I was. Four cancelled days

Detach him from us. His eyes are eyes
Not pits. He cannot prove he milked

The darkness, ran wild amid the stars.
We do not know his bed was unconfined.

Is there nothing remarkable about him?
Nothing. There is only the fact, the hard

Flawless fact. Accept it and your thoughts
Will be combed like wool. The knots reduced,

The snares shaken out. Learn his language,
Feel its stress on your own leaping pulse

And every question that you ask will burn
A fresh hole in the night. To me

He has not said a word. The fact sticks
In my throat. I cannot swallow stone.

JOHN JARMAIN [1911–1944]

Prisoners of War

Like shabby ghosts down dried-up river beds
The tired procession slowly leaves the field;
Dazed and abandoned, just a count of heads,
They file away, these who have done their last,
To that grey safety where the days are sealed,
Where no word enters, and the urgent past
Is relieved day by day against the clock
Whose hours are meaningless, whose measured rate
Brings nearer nothing, only serves to mock.

It is ended now. There's no more need to choose,
To fend and think and act; no need to hate.
Now all their will is worthless, none will lose
And none will suffer though their courage fail.
The tension in the brain is loosened now,
Its taut decisions slack: no more alone
– How I and each of us has been alone
Like lone trees which the lightnings all assail –
They are herded now and have no more to give.
Even fear is past. And death, so long so near,
Has suddenly receded to its station

In the misty end of life. For these will live,
They are quit of killing and sudden mutilation;
They no longer cower at the sound of a shell in the air,
They are safe. And in the glimmer at time's end
They will return – old, worn maybe, but sure –
And gather their bits of broken lives to mend.

HENRY TREECE [1911–1966]

Poem

What coiner carved his mark upon my heart
Before the womb forsook me, flung me to fate?
These hands that feel the future, whose are they?
Some monster strung my veins in lover's knot
And wrapped my eyes with words his father wrought
But never taught me. Whose this mad mummery?

'Who is this mocker, my maker,' I ask, 'my friend?'
Not God, whose bread explodes inside my mouth?
Pied-piper madness this benefactor loves,
Whose words of peace explode within my hand
As I offer his leaden pence for food; his truth
Fickle as breeze-twitched boughs about the eaves;

Not Time that paints his dearth upon the bough,
For death upon the rose is my death too,
Rings my heart's bells and drinks my babbling blood,
And over the salt seas blows my frail fever. Though
Tongueless, my fingers' voice attack this foe
The nagging winds, his henchmen, waste my word.

When Death has pressed his image in my face
There can be no more doubt, no more despair;
And love and loss, soft in a bed together,
Talk me a dirge meet for my fruitless age,
Laugh at my corpse, who on its broken bier
Wide-eyed with terror waits this forgotten father.

Death Mask

Hid by a stone stare, I dreamt a fox
With bloody beard: the sneering lip
Spring-hung, to kiss my hand with fang
Before the clicking second's foot could flee:
Back from the nostril's grin I watched a flower
Wither and groan, fall black upon the patient floor.

Through many dreams this hanging drum of wax
Followed my motion, waiting a slip
It seemed; and days, however long,
Led always to the dusty room, where he
Watched. By day and on the hills the power
Slept; but moon would always find him at the door.

So the thread wound: joy snapped like elder-sticks,
Brittle in winter. The thunder's clap
In silence plagued my mind; song
Shrank in the caverns of my heart. He
Tempted, till my hands snatched in their fear,
Only a spider's web, brain to the mocking leer.

Epilogue

I have come a long way from the blood's tidal voice,
Moaning and wailing across the salt flats of the mind;
A long way from the haggard priest in a twilit land
Where orchids scream in a glass-green night,
While weeping ghosts with their howling dogs
Call out to the child with flowers in his eyes.

I have moved far from the image of another
Who once walked with me, sharing one shadow;
And I have reached the prize of my own rough shroud,
Out of another's decay to my own rightful death,
And the ecstatic freedom of a personal end
Shared now with no-one and which none shall ever share.

Song for an Ending

The trees his mind planted grew fairyland pears
Away from the slag-heap and steam-organ town;
The hands he had dreamed stroked a harp's silver strings,
So he bartered his bells for a golden crown.

'Come sit on my finger you coloured birds
And sing me the song of a painted year'.
He slept in the wood where the pale moths wove
Moon's ghostly skeins through the purple air.

Like a sun he passed through the echoing halls
With a jest for the jewelled lords in his train,
Calling out to the booted messengers,
'How go my wars now in Gaul, in Spain?'

Blind, blind, and with no white friendly stick
To warn him that all men must put on grey hairs,
This stiff-booted boy in his Sunday suit,
Whistling his way through the long arched years.

Yes, the world he invented grew weary at last
And shrivelled and crumbled and fell to dust.
'You've had a good run for your money', said Now,
And a dog skipped off with the bone of his past.

O wraith of a victor, with wooden sword,
Lackland he stands in the light, poor husk,
With the ghost of his pride and ambition crying
Like a lost child's soul through the Summer dusk.

PAUL POTTS [1911–1990]

For My Father

I think a time will come when you will understand
That I was forced to try and fly and learn to sing
And that because I fell, echoless, between dark rocks
Is of itself no proof that if I had not run away
I would have grown strong and added to
The long tradition of you and your quiet sires.
Remember, too, that this emigrating is of itself
Part of your own long silent heritage.
Else, how sir, did you come to be American?

SUSANNE KNOWLES [1911–1992]

The Blitz

Hell is ours. Not in the calculated pain
We give and suffer, hate for hatred's sake,
The criminal mis-channelling of brain
Whose power is turned to break and break and break;
Future, ideas, hopes, inspiration unfulfilled
Cancelled, made vain; not in the shattered
Wretches death drops on, impersonally killed,
Their dead blood, spilt to no end, spattered
On streets; the paralysis of fear
Or the appalling race to recompense
Death with a wider death; insatiable woe,
Want, miscreation, waste. Not here, but here:
In knowing we chose this unintelligence,
In taking for granted that it could be so.

Diptych: An Annunciation

She was alone
And soon will be again:
A serious girl in a tall quiet room.
Twin arches of an unglazed window frame
A medieval town, the noonday light
Silhouettes along the sill
Small pots of musk and sage.
The virgin's red-gold hair
Is combed out to a cloak; her dress,
Her mantle, blue and blue, cascade in folds
On to the checkered marble of the floor.

An angel's interrupted her; she holds
A book half-closed – one finger keeps the page.
Robes eddying still,
The pointed peacock wings still raised
After imagined flight,
He is wholly word, irradiant.
His gravity and grace reflect her own,
His homage counters her humility.

It is their dialogue the painter shows.
There's nothing of astonishment or fear
Suggested in the young girl's downcast eyes,
The inclination of her head
And moving gesture of a slim, small hand:
The angel holds a lily
As he would a sceptre, gently blows
A little of its pollen in her ear.

MERVYN PEAKE [1911–1968]

Had Each a Voice What Would His Fingers Cry

His fingers that were trained to bind
The shadows of his mind
To paper with slim lead
Grasp grimmer substance than a pencil's measure.

Not cedar but the trigger's steel
Is what they feel,
And in a longer barrel
Lead of as fleet an impulse waits the pressure.

His perjured fingers have no throats;
His wrists no source of sound supports;
His crook'd forefinger
Curls like a tongue, severed and voice-forsaken;

Had each a voice what would his fingers cry
But 'Treachery!'?
Until their shrill pipes echoing up the arms
Should find and force the tyrant brain to hearken.

RAYNER HEPPENSTALL [1911–1981]

Instead of a Carol

The winter hardens. Every night I hear
The patient khaki beast grieve in his stall,
His eyes behind the hard fingers soft as wool.
His cheerful morning face puts me in mind
Of certain things were rumoured far and near
To hearts wherein there fretted and repined
A world that came to its last dated year.

SORLEY MACLEAN [1911–1996]

Ebb

I am not striving with the tree that will not bend for me,
and the apples will not grow on any branch;
it is not farewell to you; you have not left me.
It is the ebb of death with no floodtide after it.

Dead stream of neap in your tortured body,
which will not flow at new moon or at full,
in which the great springtide of love will not come –
but a double subsidence to lowest ebb.

Death Valley

> *Some Nazi or other has said that the Fuehrer had restored to German manhood the 'right and joy of dying in battle'.*

Sitting dead in 'Death Valley'
below the Ruweisat Ridge
a boy with his forelock down about his cheek
and his face slate-grey;

I thought of the right and the joy
that he got from his Fuehrer,
of falling in the field of slaughter
to rise no more;

of the pomp and the fame
that he had, not alone,
though he was the most piteous to see
in a valley gone to seed

with flies about grey corpses
on a dun sand
dirty yellow and full of the rubbish
and fragments of battle.

Was the boy of the band
who abused the Jews
and Communists, or of the greater
band of those

led, from the beginning of generations,
unwillingly to the trial
and mad delirium of every war
for the sake of rulers?

Whatever his desire or mishap,
his innocence or malignity,
he showed no pleasure in his death
below the Ruweisat Ridge.

FRANCIS SCARFE [1911–1986]

Progression

See that satan pollarding a tree,
That geometric man straightening a road:
Surely such passions are perverse and odd
That violate windows and set the north wind free.

No doubt tomorrow the world will be too straight,
Five hundred miles an hour will churn our dreams
Like surprised whales, when we lie a dead weight
In an ignorant sleep, and things will be what they seem.

Tomorrow we will hear on the gramophone
The Music of the Spheres, registered H.M.V.
By a divorced contralto: we shall perhaps
Meet Adam under glass in a museum
Fleshless and most unlovely, complete with pedigree.

Or else, tomorrow, workers, kings and crooks
Will all have aeroplanes and be fast friends,
In a world no longer divided by dividends,
Where love will be almost as simple as it looks.

from *No Morning*

No morning, no morning,
The sun sleeps in a cloud,
And though a hundred factories blow
Broad rings of steam and sound,

No horn will wake the worker
Back to a world of smoke,
As the city rose uncloses now
Pale in its grimy cloak.

No morning, no morning,
The worker will not wake,
For cannon spoke to cannon
Long before day-break.

SHEILA LEGGE [1911–1949]

from *I Have Done My Best For You*

And there appeared unto me a woman with chains upon her wrists, riding on a bicycle, and in her hand a banner bearing these words: THERE ARE NO MORE WHORES IN BABYLON.

'Look', she cried. 'There is the Queen Mary setting out on her maiden voyage'.

And indeed it was an impressive sight, out there in the desert, that tall ship built entirely out of the most costly marble (for no expense had been spared) setting out on her maiden voyage with her cargo of candles and all her passengers climbing up the gangway, which was made out of point de Venise and had been lent by the Pope, with their clothes and their medicine bottles neatly packed in rooks' nests and a ham sandwich for the journey.

MAX CHAPMAN [1911–1999]

Night Fruit

One death
    for each known petal;
five of blood
    and five of metal.

Pick, till day
    lets mutely fall
a fanwise curtain
    for her pall,

and springly love treads
    round the bend
to an utter and
    insidious end.

For each known petal
    each known death –
and a moth-measure
    of shrunken breath.

ROBERT PAYNE [1911–1983]

Dido

Darling, I did not know
That you were like that queen
Who died so long ago
Upon a flaming pyre.
O Dido, Queen of Tyre,
Of all things seen and unseen
You were the loveliest:
But when I saw you go
By candlelight to bed,
I saw your throat on fire
And your white fingers bled,
The flames were in your hair,
Your screaming mouth was red.
I beg the fire to spare
The loveliest and the best
From the consuming dead,
From darkness and the beast.

ANNE RIDLER [1912–2001]

The Crab

The crab is in again, his monthly house
Open and loth, patient only of force;
Here he huddles on my back, the pools
That three weeks hid him, after the queasy pale
Swept up my path before him, washed him to me.
Kings feeding fat, clogged rivers on the plain,
Or choked with stars the dark, as all satiety
I feel him, clutching there, while each capacity
Goes to enlarge him; dance the pincers of pain,
My self flies rook up to watch, afraid of the din,
Sings to cover it, yet hears and rooted feels.

Any day beats by, force accepted, heals
Nightly homing the Monday gloom of an office –
If you can say it heals that turns from brass
Bitter to stealing hope in the mind a knowledge
In facts unchanged. So as with the anxious,
This wasteful process can seem gentle to us,
Flown out in peace all the disgust of blood and illness.
For we take comfort in any achievement, even a courage
That could not be refused: this inner success
May weight circumstance to temporary peace.
Even the periodic cancer need not distress us,
Could we but keep the peace and lose the venomous.

Bunhill Fields

Under cool trees the City tombs
　　　Extend, and nearer lie
Stones above Blake's and Bunyan's bones
　　　To Vivian's working days than I.

Since he is gentle, wild and good
　　　As you were, peaceable Shades,
There may he go within your care
　　　As in my heart his love resides.

Such a care as held unharmed
　　　The three within the fire;
Spread wings like those that led
　　　Tobias in the dangerous shire.

And if I fear his death too much,
　　　Let me not learn more faith
By sad trial of what I dread,
　　　Nor grieve him by my own death.

For our faith is one which may
　　　Convert but not console;
We shall not, except by our own will,
　　　Part for ever in the gape of hell.

Kirkwall 1942

Far again, far,
And the Pentland howling psalms of separation
Lifts and falls, lifts and falls between.
But present pain

Folds like a firth round islets that contain
A sheepfold and a single habitation –
Moments in our summer of success –
Or the greater islands, colonised and built with peace.

Cold knives of light
Make every outline clear in a northern island,
The separating light, the sea's green;
Yet southern lives
Merge in the lupin fields or sleepy coves,
In crowstepped gables find a hint of Holland,
And Europe in the red religious stone:
All places in the room where we in love lie down.

JOHN SINGER [C 1912–1950]

And No Tale Told

And no tale told, the flesh is a deceiver
a dry-eyed death invents, and no word wept
where minutes rant, and no green dream, and no insistent whisper,
and no brief morrow.

And no calm lust, the hour unveils the flower
the flame invites, and no implicit noon
in your heart's wrath, and no indulgencies
when priest is bankrupt.

And no green leaf can make the earth a pillow
for finished rakes, no gathering the blossom
whose leaves are dark, whose fruit is seek-tomorrow,

whose stem is supple with the oil of midnight,
whose ravishing is sleep, alone, alive,
and no love lost.

Ballad

Earth made the ballad and the fruits carried it.
Thrush and thresher married it.
Wheat and winepress were its children
And greed harried it.

Earth made the ballad in a day of reaping
Sweat and sweetness crowned it.
Liberty, dying, downed it.
But the ballad lived through a day of weeping.

Man made the ballad in an hour of knowing.
When labour levelled and lifted
And battling slew and sifted
And the infant, brotherhood, a long time growing.

Time made the ballad with its heart in labour.
Gold delayed it, fear waylaid it,
Power crushed and cynicism flayed it,
But the ballad sung itself alive again,
For courage was its heart, need its will,
And commonsense its neighbour.

J.F. HENDRY [1912–1986]

Apocalypse

Who are the speaking wound
And world thrust stride over death,
Star burred with symbols and
The blind ghost shaping fountain's
Horror strewn with mind
Through the talking fiend?

A cloud-skull strangling sun
A spine-haired cannibal sky
Stabs the blown heart green. Man
Polared east of sex and west
Of death crowns iron
Orbits with a bone.

Husk, skeleton and cyst-
Wounds manacle the frozen child
From blood and furnace. Thrust
World's a fig for rankling age,
And shadows beam the ghost
They shed, forever fast

By shriven marrow-
Blowing bone to trumpet stick
Of eye through sunspot pores.
The-devil-wounds-the-burrowing-
Angel, barbed with blood, blares
Many the wireworm war.

Picasso – for Guernica

Frozen in the fright of light chilled skull and spine
Drip bone-shriek-splinters sharper than the Bren:
Starve franco stroke and stave the hooves of bulls.
I am the arm thrust candle through the wall.

Up cities crack firelaughter, the furious
Minutes, and bark a ruin at man in
His sealoneliness, hair rearing finrays.
I am the spinning coil distilled eyes' iron.

Neigh, horse, terror through steel teeth and a thicket
Of bricks! Beam an eyebomb, cellar, and stride
Nerve, peeled pupil's enamel, rhomboid head!
I am the tiled blind hand plunged bulb in socket.

Splint for the shriven shin I foster mantrump out
Of festered history; sprout pointed fingers
Where an afterbirth is dung and rubble-teat.
I am the eyeball blown world! Axis of anger!

London Before Invasion, 1940

Walls and buildings stand here still, like shells,
Hold them to the ear. There are no echoes even
Of the seas that once were. That tide is out
Beyond the valleys and hills.

Days dawn and die, while the city assumes a distance of stars.
It is the absence of the heart
In the ebbing seas of heaven,
An ebbing beyond laughter and too tense for tears.

Now, imagination floats, a weed, on water's vacancy.
Faces of women, lit with conscience past or future
Of men gone, wear one garland of stone features.
Flowers have a girl's irrelevance, and mind is no prescience.

Flood-tides returning may bring with them blood and fire,
Blenching with wet panic spirit that must be rock.
May bring a future tossed and torn, as slippery as wrack.
All time adrift in torrents of blind war.

Midnight Air-Raid

Beyond our factories, like caterpillars curled in a sham death,
Rivers signal their quicksilver treachery: and, in answer,
The guns of midnight pound from roots of earth
Bombarding with their radium mouth and prong of cancer
Eating out the lungs of countries in a bubble of bloody breath.

Sensitive fingers of searchlights pick the pockets of dark.
These are surgeon's pitiless forceps imprisoning in their grip
Anaerobic death, there, in the heart of air, lurking
To burst the harmless tissues of cities. It is an antisepsis
In this world of blood, with an unsuspecting child, the dawn, forgotten larks.

Now sirens unleash civilian anguish. In a reflex, they
Stumble from an underworld of dreams whom abortive desire
(Pillared in moonlit limbs) makes gray.
Freedom's involuntary fighters, knowing no refuge save in fiery
Consciousness, rampant light and the resolution of day.

Night that sealed their visions, drained all thought an hour
Ago, is now their bodyguard; but real defence is an illumination,
Ally of the sun, and fills their brain with staggering power

Where sanity tremors on madness, to beat down explosion
Of wind and the thunder's stupor, in a turbulent underground anger.

Here artist and scientist concur to admire
A formal pattern of battle, where herring-bone squadrons
Elude the swaying bars of light, and white fire
From London's living furnace, flung up like a tilted cauldron,
Splits the atom of doom; and makes man's floodlit march one endless
gyre.

Churchillian Ode

The years grew tares for we did not tend them.
Time was eaten by moths in an age of gold
And the sun eclipsed in a cloud of ignorance.
The hours sprang holes as we stared, until now, the last,
We clasp in our hands a sheaf of bluebells in place
Of the rifle, and all our moments of laughter are frozen
Amid flaming towns, their echoes chill as the shadow of soul's
vengeance.

I bring you no song, no troubadour, but a hymn
Of embattled fury and anthems of fortitude to beat back
Piebald panic, calculation's treachery, lunacy's assault,
The seven fretful seas of disloyalty and abdication in high places.
I offer you inspiration in crates of munitions. My poems are
Cool water to drink in bomb-craters. I erect wires of barbed
Speech in action to cripple the deliberate hunter of human freedom.

You will pardon us, Hitler, if perhaps our laughter is red.
If your soldiers, laughing with us, choke, and halt
As the blood bubbles trumpets in their throats. You will
Certainly pardon the laughter you launched as slaughter.

We still have a mind toward sun and essential joy, although
Giants carouse and skirl on our reeling horizon's fire.
You will pardon this soldier's Belgian doll, and those who fought in flowers.

I might recite the names of cities with the culture of the tongues
Of centuries: Wien: Praha: Warszawa: Rotterdam: towns murdered
Like fair women by a cut-purse snuffling the crumbs of ruin,
Recite to no purpose. For Amiens burns today and Paris tomorrow.
Time is afire with terror in the forest of our streets and
Eloquence marshals clearings arresting death's advance,
Cuts channels, floods dykes, builds a citadel for a people in arms.

Though all the air is calamitous with weeping, O Hitler,
Silt of your wreckage, an ambition's debacle, and the debris
Piles inanity upon insanity too torn for the mind to understand –
Yet I hear our horns at sea blare troopships.
I listen where whispers of victory drown the sirens of anguish,
And through the fog of murderous dreams
Drifting up, acrid and brown, I see the merciful,
Miraculous dissolution of bombast and lust, in an elemental Marlborough.

LAWRENCE DURRELL [1912–1990]

The Poet

Time marched against my egg,
But Saturn hatched it:
Furnished two rusty claws,
The antelope's logic:
While by the turtle's coma in summer
The new moon watched it.

Four seasons conspired
To poison my water: with scissors
A late spring lanced the bud,
Tightened the caul on my skull,
Lulled me in dragon's blood.

Sun withered this crucible head,
Wove me by a tragical loom.
Nine moons heard of my coming,
The drumming of mythical horses
On the walls of the womb.

Winter buried the eyes like talents.
Tightened the temple's bony ring,
And now the pie is opened,
Feathered the head of the owlet –
What shall the monster sing?

Paris Journal: For David Gascoyne (1939)

Monday escapes destruction.
Record a vernal afternoon,
Tea on the lawn with mother,
A parochial interest in love, etc.
By the deviation of a hair,
Is death so far, so far, no further.

Tuesday: visibility good: and Wednesday.
A little thunder, some light showers.
A library book about the universe.
The absence of a definite self.
O and already by Friday hazardous,
To Saturday begins the slow reverse.
A Saturday without form. By midnight
The equinox seems forever gone:
Yet the motionless voice repeating:
'Bless the hills in paradigms of smoke,
Manhair, Maidenhair meeting'.

But today Sunday. The pit.
The axe and the knot. Cannot write.
The monster in its booth.
At a quarter to one the mask repeating:
'Truth is what is
Truth is what is Truth?'

DONAGH MACDONAGH [1912–1968]

A Parable

Envious of the birds the father gathers
Wings from the wind, wings from the mind
And feathers limb and thought until
The sky can bear him lightly and
Lift him above his day. The son
Eye-tethered runs and cheers the daring
Conqueror until his fingers
Soften in feathers and his voice
Becomes a strangled sea-call. Then
Daedalus and his son rejoice together
While naiads underwave already
Weep for the birds that had been men.

SEÁN JENNETT [1912–1981]

Mahoney

Then Mahoney, standing in the surf,
the convoy hanging in the misty sea
and landing forces moving up the beach,
dropped down his arms, and said
I wait, O god, I wait,
and these were his last words of common speech.

Christ in the shallows of the water walked
or in the sweaty hollow of his palm
appeared and spoke to his reluctant bone

or moved about the chambers of his skull,
the scourger of the temple, with a whip;
and in his heart also the lash had been.

So Mahoney stood and let his rifle fall
into the sea, where lug-worms claimed it, and
the servant tide; and heard his captain shout,
but did not move; and felt the weight of wheels
and tracks across the cortex of his brain;
but did not certainly hear the single shot.

Wife, children, parents, weep for him, who now
dead with the grey crabs and the starfish rests
where surges heap on him the slow and secret sand.
Yet even in the valleys of the sea
the dead can feel the libel, and Mahoney
in his stripped skull is tortured by a lie.

BRENDA CHAMBERLAIN [1912–1971]

Dead Ponies

There is death enough in Europe without these
dead ponies on the mountain.
(They are the underlining, the emphasis of death.)
It is not wonderful that when they live
their eyes are shadowed under mats of hair.
Despair and famine do not gripe so hard
when the bound earth and sky are kept remote
behind clogged hairs.

The snows engulfed them, pressed their withered haunches flat,
filled up their nostrils, burdened the cage of their ribs.

The snow retreated. Their bodies stink to heaven,
potently crying out to raven, hawk, and dog,
Come pick us clean, cleanse our fine bones of blood.

They were never lovely save as foals
before their necks grew long, uncrested;
but the wildness of the mountain was in their stepping,
the pride of Spring burnt in their haunches;
they were tawny as the rushes of the marsh.

The prey-birds have had their fill and preen their feathers:
soft entrails have gone to make the hawk arrogant.

GEORGE WOODCOCK [1912–1995]

Conscientious Objectors

The icy, empty dawn cracks in the fields
Under the labouring feet. Two cross the grass
With slashers on their shoulders sloped like guns,
Drawing dark lines in rime white as they pass.

Standing in filthy ditches in leaking boots
They fell the towering hedges like Jericho walls
Under the blast of day. Around their feet
The numbing water seeps through invisible holes.

Strange they have come from library and office.
Hands that have felt no toil, myopic eyes
And sloping backs revolt from an alien time.
Under a dead sky they expiate their oddness.

Having left friends and substitutes for love
In the leaning fragments of a distant city
They tread the furrows of infertile fields
And return to their pasts in a wet country.

Over their ineffectual misery, their boredom
And the empty sequence of unprivate days
The lost shadows of the city become their end.
The cause that brought them dwindles. They hate blank skies,

The biting wind and the black bones of trees,
The promise of spring as a green omen of toil.
They rest their slashers and talk of a starlit town
As the weak sun breaks on the land without a hill.

PAUL DEHN [1912–1976]

Armistice

It is finished. The enormous dust-cloud over Europe
Lifts like a million swallows; and a light,
Drifting in craters, touches the quiet dead.

Now, at the bugle's hour, before the blood
Cakes in a clean wind on their marble faces,
Making them monuments; before the sun

Hung like a medal on the smoky noon,
Whitens the bone that feeds the earth; before
Wheat-ear springs green, again, in the green spring

And they are bread in the bodies of the young:
Be strong to remember how the bread died, screaming;
Gangrene was corn, and monuments went mad.

F.T. PRINCE [1912–2003]

False Bay

She I love leaves me, and I leave my friends
In the dusky capital where I spent two years
In the cultivation of divinity.
Sitting beside my window above the sea
In this unvisited land I feel once more
How little ingenious I am. The winter ends,
The seaward slopes are covered to the shore
With a press of lilies that have silver ears.
And although I am perplexed and sad, I say
'Now indulge in no dateless lamentations;
Watch only across the water the lapsed nations
And the fishermen twitch a boat across the bay'.

Soldiers Bathing

The sea at evening moves across the sand.
Under a reddening sky I watch the freedom of a band
Of soldiers who belong to me. Stripped bare
For bathing in the sea, they shout and run in the warm air;

Their flesh, worn by the trade of war, revives
And my mind towards the meaning of it strives.

All's pathos now. The body that was gross,
Rank, ravenous, disgusting in the act or in repose,
All fever, filth and sweat, its bestial strength
And bestial decay, by pain and labour grows at length
Fragile and luminous. 'Poor bare forked animal',
Conscious of his desires and needs and flesh that rise and fall,
Stands in the soft air, tasting after toil
The sweetness of his nakedness: letting the sea-waves coil
Their frothy tongues about his feet, forgets
His hatred of the war, its terrible pressure that begets
A machinery of death and slavery,
Each being a slave and making slaves of others: finds that he
Remembers lovely freedom in a game,
Mocking himself, and comically mimics fear and shame.

He plays with death and animality.
And reading in the shadows of his pallid flesh, I see
The idea of Michelangelo's cartoon
Of soldiers bathing, breaking off before they were half done
At some sortie of the enemy, an episode
Of the Pisan wars with Florence. I remember how he showed
Their muscular limbs that clamber from the water,
And heads that turn across the shoulder, eager for the slaughter,
Forgetful of their bodies that are bare,
And hot to buckle on and use the weapons lying there.
– And I think too of the theme another found
When, shadowing men's bodies on a sinister red ground,
Another Florentine, Pollaiuolo,
Painted a naked battle: warriors, straddled, hacked the foe,
Dug their bare toes into the ground and slew

The brother-naked man who lay between their feet and drew
His lips back from his teeth in a grimace.

They were Italians who knew war's sorrow and disgrace
And showed the thing suspended, stripped: a theme
Born out of the experience of war's horrible extreme
Beneath a sky where even the air flows
With *lacrimae Christi*. For that rage, that bitterness, those blows,
That hatred of the slain, what could they be
But indirectly or directly a commentary
On the Crucifixion? And the picture burns
With indignation and pity and despair by turns,
Because it is the obverse of the scene
Where Christ hangs murdered, stripped, upon the Cross. I mean,
That is the explanation of its rage.

And we too have our bitterness and pity that engage
Blood, spirit in this war. But night begins,
Night of the mind: who nowadays is conscious of our sins?
Though every human deed concerns our blood,
And even we must know, what nobody has understood,
That some great love is over all we do,
And that is what has driven us to this fury, for so few
Can suffer all the terror of that love:
The terror of that love has set us spinning in this groove
Greased with our blood.

These dry themselves and dress,
Combing their hair, forget the fear and shame of nakedness.
Because to love is frightening we prefer
The freedom of our crimes. Yet, as I drink the dusky air,
I feel a strange delight that fills me full,
Strange gratitude, as if evil itself were beautiful,
And kiss the wound in thought, while in the west
I watch a streak of red that might have issued from Christ's breast.

CHARLES MADGE [1912–1996]

To a Mermaid: I

The glass entanglement of flowery hair
Deceives a plane. Because the looking glass
Creates the metaphoric double there

Undoubted image. Not less perfect was,
They say, a face once found in television
Bent by the hills, perspective of a face,

Hardest to catch with exigent precision,
Indeed stone cold. The limper, could he climb
Down backstairs aboriginal incision?

Or should he racing get his stitch in time
For hemming her green flood who rose, while spate
Flowed foam? (The lights, the lights of evening shine,

Search, cliff to cliff, pharos, and swimmers late)
Or dredge up the lost gold of Hellespont?
Or crystal nugget hew of hardest fate?

Enchanted difficulty is what we want
To make from the loved stone, and to endure,
As in the welling measure of the fount,
Until the exhaustion of the sandy shore.

ROY FULLER [1912–1991]

What is Terrible

Life at last I know is terrible:
The innocent scene, the innocent walls and light
And hills for me are like the cavities
Of surgery or dreams. The visible might
Vanish, for all it reassures, in white.

This apprehension has come slowly to me,
Like symptoms and bulletins of sickness. I
Must first be moved across two oceans, then
Bored, systematically and sickeningly,
In a place where war is news. And constantly

I must be threatened with what is certainly worse:
Peril and death, but no less boring. And
What else? Besides my fear, my misspent time,
My love, hurt and postponed, there is the hand
Moving the empty glove; the bland

Aspect of nothing disguised as something; that
Part of living incommunicable,
For which we try to find vague adequate
Images, and which, after all,
Is quite surprisingly communicable.

Because in the clear hard light of war the ghosts
Are seen to be suspended by wires, and in
The old house the attic is empty: and the furious
Inner existence of objects and even
Ourselves is largely a myth: and for the sin

To blame our fathers, to attribute vengeance
To the pursuing chorus, and to live
In a good and tenuous world of private values,
Is simply to lie when only truth can give
Continuation in time to bread and love.

For what is terrible is the obvious
Organisation of life: the oiled black gun,
And what it cost, the destruction of Europe by
Its councils; the unending justification
Of that which cannot be justified, what is done.

The year, the month, the day, the minute, at war
Is terrible and my participation
And that of all the world is terrible.
My living now must bear the laceration
Of the herd, and always will. What's done

To me is done to many. I can see
No ghosts, but only the fearful actual
Lives of my comrades. If the empty whitish
Horror is ever to be flushed and real,
It must be for them and changed by them all.

ELIZABETH SMART [1913–1986]

Song: The Singing Summer Streets

Nothing dies, it bursts to birth
Before the requiem is half done,
Before the suitable tears are shed
Or the mourning of the underbred
Nags out its course, the death is dead.

The sighs shoot into the loud trombone
It blows so hard it shakes the earth.
The flowers in a breathless rush break through;
If one has collapsed then out spring two,
Insatiable for things to do.

It is unnecessary to atone
For sin: he is the losing one;
With all his conjuror's cheap disguise
No geese fly north because of his lies,
No cause is lost, and nothing dies.

GEORGE BARKER [1913–1991]

from *Calamiterror Book I*

1

What when born upward breaking from heaven downward
It is my bare bloodred babe, with beauty
Branching from armpit, maypole at thigh, world flying
Like fairboats around, the axis of existence.
The bud beginning, the burning salamander
Suspended in his breast, the shambles in the bowels,
The tall tree spine supporting vertical
The crucified to life bare body blood.

2

The eye-shaped leaf, the topmost of the tree,
Examines heaven, the leaf-shaped eye examines
The eye-shaped leaf, and each observes in each
Heaven and heaven. I have observed the leaf
Flying like bird over mountains carrying in its curve
The brainstruck eyeball. Whither I cry
And the tongue leaf lifts its tongue,
Somewhere O somewhere where the summer month
Builds a green body of leaf about the bone.

Holy Poems (C.B. in memoriam. June, MCMXXXIX): IV: i

I am Saint John on Patmos of my heart
Towered and tabernacled with illusion;
Black Michaels and gold Satans stand at hand
Gulling me with their gestures of temptation

To bring me down from the marvellous mountains
Where in Babylonian gardens I find
Spinoza's face hanging from every tree
Murmuring love of all our kith and kind:
Or I feel, cold as a draught on my arm,
The spiralling universe like a worm
Coiling for comfort; and in my mind
The three-winged dove among my dreams
Moaning for its apocalyptic home.

To W.S. Graham

Shuffle the empires and pacify their sons
But still toothed rage goes sabring the lambs
Where they stroll in a twilight of myrtle. Break
Her sleeping heart with an Ajax fist
And she, my lifelong love, dovetongued and bright,
Will sleep with me, for I can patch her pitcher
Enfountain it, fold, hold, and befriend it.
Jock, you with the golden fleece on your sleeve,
Where's the heart, man, for the egoed sea to shatter
Sea against rock of heart? She is my love
Whom with your five-fingered hammer you tear
To an anger of poems. In the straking night
The mermaid with immortality in her hair
Will rise to you the hour you sink to her.

from *The True Confession of George Barker*

Come, sulking woman, bare as water,
        Dazzle me now as you dazzled me
When, blinded by your nudity,

I saw the sex of the intellect,
The idea of the beautiful.
The beautiful to which I, later,
Gave only mistrust and neglect,
The idea no dishonour can annul.

Vanquished aviatrix, descend
Again, long vanished vision whom
I have not known so long, assume
Your former bright prerogative,
Illuminate, guide and attend
Me now. O living vision, give
The grace, the verity; and send
The spell that makes the poem live.

[...]

Star-fingered shepherdess of Sleep
Come, pacify regret, remorse;
And let the suffering black sheep
Weep on the bed it made. Let pause
The orphic criminal to perceive
That in the venue of his days
All the crimes look back and grieve
Over lies no grief allays.

Sleep at my side again, my bride,
As on our marriage bed you turned
Into a flowering bush that burned
All the proud flesh away. Beside
Me now, you, shade of my departed
Broken, abandoned bride, lie still,
And I shall hold you close until
Even our ghosts are broken-hearted.

R.S. THOMAS [1913–2000]

Maes-yr-Onnen

Though I describe it stone by stone, the chapel
Left stranded in the hurrying grass,
Painting faithfully the mossed tiles and the tree,
The one listener to the long homily
Of the ministering wind, and the dry, locked doors,
And the stale piety, mouldering within:
You cannot share with me the rarer air,
Blue as a flower and heady with the scent
Of the years past and others yet to be,
That brushed each window and outsoared the clouds'
Far foliage with its own high canopy.
You cannot hear as I, incredulous, heard
Up in the rafters, where the bell should ring,
The wild, sweet singing of Rhiannon's birds.

EDWARD LOWBURY [1913–2007]

August 10th, 1945: The Day After

Who will be next to break this terrible silence,
While the doom of war still shivers over these
Unwilling either to die or to be defeated, –
In the agony of death still torn, contorted,
Torn between saving face and body, both
Mutilated almost beyond recognition?
The face fights on long after
The body's overwhelmed and hacked to pieces.
Every scar of it's their fault; yet I am dumb;

In the blind eyes of pity the good and the evil
Are equals when they're gasping in the sand,
Helpless. The reality so blinds
Our senses that it seems less than a dream,
Yet we shall live to say 'Twice in a lifetime
We saw such nakedness that shame
Itself could not look on, and of all the feelings,
Hate, anger, justice, vengeance, violence, –
Horror alone remained, its organ voice
Searching us with a sickening clarity'.
And now the word comes in of those two cities
With all their living burden
Blown to the wind by power
Unused except by God at the creation, –
Atomised in the flash of an eye.
Who else but God or the instrument of God
Has power to pass such sentence?
Here the road forks, to survival or extinction,
And I hold my tongue through the awful silence,
For if God had nothing to do with it,
Extinction is the least price man can pay.

DYLAN THOMAS [1914–1953]

Before I knocked

Before I knocked and flesh let enter,
With liquid hands tapped on the womb,
I who was as shapeless as the water
That shaped the Jordan near my home
Was brother to Mnetha's daughter
And sister to the fathering worm.

I who was deaf to spring and summer,
Who knew not sun nor moon by name,
Felt thud beneath my flesh's armour,
As yet was in a molten form,
The leaden stars, the rainy hammer,
Swung by my father from his dome.

I knew the message of the winter,
The darted hail, the childish snow,
And the wind was my sister suitor;
Wind in me leaped, the hellborn dew;
My veins flowed with the Eastern weather;
Ungotten I knew night and day.

As yet ungotten, I did suffer;
The rack of dreams my lily bones
Did twist into a living cipher,
And flesh was snipped to cross the lines
Of gallow crosses on the liver
And brambles in the wringing brains.

My throat knew thirst before the structure
Of skin and vein around the well
Where words and water make a mixture
Unfailing till the blood runs foul;
My heart knew love, my belly hunger;
I smelt the maggot in my stool.

And time cast forth my mortal creature
To drift or drown upon the seas
Acquainted with the salt adventure
Of tides that never touch the shores.
I who was rich was made the richer
By sipping at the vine of days.

I, born of flesh and ghost, was neither
A ghost nor man, but mortal ghost.
And I was struck down by death's feather.
I was a mortal to the last
Long breath that carried to my father
The message of his dying christ.

You who bow down at cross and altar,
Remember me and pity Him
Who took my flesh and bone for armour
And doublecrossed my mother's womb.

The force that through the green fuse

The force that through the green fuse drives the flower
Drives my green age; that blasts the roots of trees
Is my destroyer.
And I am dumb to tell the crooked rose
My youth is bent by the same wintry fever.

The force that drives the water through the rocks
Drives my red blood; that dries the mouthing streams
Turns mine to wax.
And I am dumb to mouth unto my veins
How at the mountain spring the same mouth sucks.

The hand that whirls the water in the pool
Stirs the quicksand; that ropes the blowing wind
Hauls my shroud sail.
And I am dumb to tell the hanging man
How of my clay is made the hangman's lime.

The lips of time leech to the fountain head;
Love drips and gathers, but the fallen blood
Shall calm her sores.
And I am dumb to tell a weather's wind
How time has ticked a heaven round the stars.

And I am dumb to tell the lover's tomb
How at my sheet goes the same crooked worm.

A Refusal to Mourn the Death, by Fire, of a Child in London

Never until the mankind making
Bird beast and flower
Fathering and all humbling darkness
Tells with silence the last light breaking
And the still hour
Is come of the sea tumbling in harness

And I must enter again the round
Zion of the water bead
And the synagogue of the ear of corn

Shall I let pray the shadow of a sound
Or sow my salt seed
In the least valley of sackcloth to mourn

The majesty and burning of the child's death.
I shall not murder
The mankind of her going with a grave truth
Nor blaspheme down the stations of the breath
With any further
Elegy of innocence and youth.

Deep with the first dead lies London's daughter,
Robed in the long friends,
The grains beyond age, the dark veins of her mother,
Secret by the unmourning water
Of the riding Thames.
After the first death, there is no other.

RUTHVEN TODD [1914–1978]

Worm Interviewed

It said it was the resurrection's worm
Coiling its long whip in the empty vein;
Again, it said, I am the carnal worm
Sprung sweetly from the tissue of the head;
I, and I only, know the marrows of the brain,
The mysterious tissue of the infertile egg.

I caused the mind storm in the summer,
Throwing my long spear in the blood;

I caused the cracking of the missing rib,
My teeth the chisel and my eye the hammer.
Being the maggot in the newly dead
I heard the last pulse come bitterly.

I stole the tendon from the fractured foot
As scaffolding to bolster up my nest;
I stole the nerve that held the eye to socket,
Now dropped aimlessly upon the cheek.
I was the asp about the virgin's breast
That made the milk to run at Christmas time.

I was the first thing and am the last;
I made the bone that cowered in the womb,
My nest about it made the firm hard limb.
I am the maker who does not count the cost
Of the long shelter of the tomb.
I am the priest who battens on the dead.

After a Defeat

So, in the end, seeing no chance of victory,
I fled along the old road to the shore,
Round by the column standing on the downs –
Remnant of Chirico beside the bitter sea.
Memorial of ground where once before
Men fought, it kept its armoury of bone
Secure against the changes of the weather.

Those who pursued me now, keen on the chase,
Had studied out the paths for many years,
Safeguarded against the desperate survivor.
But they forgot this was my native place:

The gaping hedgerows and the snaring wires
Were no traps to me who knew the badger's lair
And the leveret's hollows in the heather.

Sheltered by bracken on the steepest cliff,
I saw them pass below me and I heard
The thresh of rifle-butts among the hazel,
The heartening shout and the high, strained laugh,
And the quick shot fired at a startled bird.
Till in the evening I saw them slowly leave,
Mocked by the column and the sharp-eyed weasel.

EITHNE WILKINS [1914–1975]

from *For Those Who Are Alive*

Cloaked in destruction, in the rocks and flames, in roll of drums,
with earnest tread of some long funeral with flags and drums,
they go: a cold wind rising, and the gulls flying
inland, and the banners crying
all that lost grandeur of the future wars,
a thud and splash
of dark floods underground, lapping
about the mourners as they march.
And the flames of darkness lean, as steeples toppling over,
and the city houses fall slowly towards the ground.
Under a hush of clouds they pass: a smoking torch,
the black sky climbing
from the estuary, a storm
that will not break till night has closed upon them.

And heavily as a coffin, in its shroud,
some presence here rings in
the waiting crowds.
Heavy the presence in the coming stone, the sculptor's mass
from which to chisel out the ghost, the eye in flames.

Such was Swift, whose mind
fled from the hammerings of the will, the dreadful flesh,
and that old gambler with the overshadowing angel and the frantic poor,
their medals pawned in Moscow,
such was François Villon too, when drunk with thirty years of shame
he saw necessity a wolf come leaping out of twilit woods.
All walked the edge of that abyss
not many speak of, and which is
as simple as a bullet through the brain.
And all, among them once the dour Beethoven, on the world's horizon, in
a darkening world,
from where the will streamed endlessly away
as men may bleed to death,
died with their fists clenched in the empty pockets,
who lived with roofless eyes, a trial of strength against the unknown
frontiers,
and had their conversations with the earthworm and the scowling eagle
that shouts across the open grave.

Now they are rid
of what by inches killed them,
their terrible prophetic pains and love.
Bare as Stonehenge,
they are burnt down to dry bone:
their skulls aswim with light, drinking and talking the long waves of light,
their invisible talk grammarless, they whirl out like bugles.

And on natural earth
only their violent fingers prod like stones,
the spade strikes rock.
And then the mourners may start back
with looks behind them,
lashed by the darkening flags, the thunder closing in,
and rave against each other, suddenly with guns, and frantic in a
 dream of death.

LAURIE LEE [1914–1997]

Thistle

Thistle, blue bunch of daggers
rattling upon the wind,
saw-tooth that separates
the lips of grasses.

Your wound in childhood was
a savage shock of joy
that set the bees on fire
and the loud larks singing.

Your head enchanted then
smouldering among the flowers
filled the whole sky with smoke
and sparks of seed.

Now from your stabbing bloom's
nostalgic point of pain
ghosts of those summers rise
rustling across my eyes.

Seeding a magic thorn
to prick the memory,
to start in my icy flesh
fevers of long lost fields.

The Edge of Day

The dawn's precise pronouncement waits
With breath of light indrawn,
Then forms with smoky, smut-red lips
The great O of the sun.

The mouldering atoms of the dark
Blaze into morning air;
The birdlike stars droop down and die,
The starlike birds catch fire.

The thrush's tinder throat strikes up,
The sparrow chips hot sparks
From flinty tongue, and all the sky
Showers with electric larks.

And my huge eye a chaos is
Where molten worlds are born;
Where floats the eagle's flaming moon,
And crows, like clinkers, burn;

Where blackbirds scream with comet tails,
And flaring finches fall,
And starlings, aimed like meteors,
Bounce from the garden wall;

Where, from the edge of day I spring
Alive for mortal flight,
Lit by the heart's exploding sun
Bursting from night to night.

C.H. SISSON [1914–2003]

A Letter to John Donne

On 27 July 1617, John Donne preached at the parish church at Sevenoaks, of which he was rector, and was entertained at Knole, then the country residence of Richard Sackville, third Earl of Dorset.

I understand you well enough, John Donne
First, that you were a man of ability
Eaten by lust and by the love of God
Then, that you crossed the Sevenoaks High Street
As rector of Saint Nicholas:
I am of that parish.

To be a man of ability is not much
You may see them on the Sevenoaks platform any day
Eager men with despatch cases
Whom ambition drives as they drive the machine
Whom the certainty of meticulous operation
Pleasures as a morbid sex a heart of stone.

That you should have spent your time in the corruption of courts
As these in that of cities, gives you no place among us:
Ability is not even the game of a fool

But the click of a computer operating in a waste
Your cleverness is dismissed from the suit
Bring out your genitals and your theology.

What makes you familiar is this dual obsession;
Lust is not what the rutting stag knows
It is to take Eve's apple and to lose
The stag's paradisal look:
The love of God comes readily
To those who have most need.

You brought body and soul to this church
Walking there through the park alive with deer
But now what animal has climbed into your pulpit?
One whose pretension is that the fear
Of God has heated him into a spirit
An evaporated man no physical ill can hurt.

Well might you hesitate at the Latin gate
Seeing such apes denying the church of God:
I am grateful particularly that you were not a saint
But extravagant whether in bed or in your shroud.
You would understand that in the presence of folly
I am not sanctified but angry.

Come down and speak to the men of ability
On the Sevenoaks platform and tell them
That at your Saint Nicholas the faith
Is not exclusive in the fools it chooses
That the vain, the ambitious and the highly sexed
Are the natural prey of the incarnate Christ.

PETER YATES [BORN 1914]

The Cube of Now

No bird of volted eye
Sky crashing grief
Will splinter this
Dead word of life,
No rocket of high fever
Ever bursting bars
Mounting out of this
Eye-socket shooting stars
Will journey out of this
Dense cube of now.

The Double Door

In arrogance of Art the traps are manned
To make immobile His quick wraith.
            Desolate is the eye of faith;
                        And none may understand
Why in rude oaths or in the exhaled breath
Of flowers, He enters and goes out of mind.

Saints walk on water by His afterglow;
Yet thought compels the fallen one
            Who burns in glory like the sun,
                        Teaching what all may know:
A darker prince, whose enmity with God
Makes poems grow, and gives sweet heat to love.

This dark prince triumphs on the siren coast;
And in his coiled and cobra sting
    The Eve kiss haunts us, and we sing
        Forgetful of that Ghost
Who on the water of love's might-have-been
Bids us still follow, and not fear to drown.

Let corn and flowers brush the needy hand;
We do with bodies we are lent;
    Love turns upon this argument.
        And love may understand
Who gives the pain, and why a lifetime burns
A blowlamp on the double door of death.

NORMAN NICHOLSON [1914–1987]

Now in the Time of This Mortal Life

Frost is tight upon the land
Constricts it with a bony hand,
Yet with blade as sharp as a nail
The immanent crocus drills the soil.
Man's nerves aver his spinal wish
And feel the Word becoming Flesh.

God watches soil and spirit mated,
And consecrates what he created,
By raising manhood unto God,
By raising raisins unto blood;
The sacramental prongs reach down
And lift earth to the skies again.
Incarnate God shines brighter than

Flower or frost, or sea or sun.
The Spirit in the limbs of man
Hardens like a skeleton,
And the earth feels a new life burrow
Along its stony bones like marrow.
For now the ritual seed is sown
To grow the stalk to bear the grain
To yield the flour to make the bread
That sinful hands shall turn to God.

The hooks of love are in our limbs
And hoist through the scholastic times
When bursting bud and bomb deny
The Manichaean heresy.
And man finds voice to curse once more
The evil in the holy fear,
And man finds heart to praise again
The hope within the evil pain.
Christ-knife heals the wound it prunes,
And carves its gospel on the bones,
That man may hear what God has heard,
And feel the Flesh becoming Word.

AUDREY BEECHAM [1915–1989]

Exile

A wind like this tonight
For such a one:
To clutch his throat
And bind with ice-thongs tight.

A shower of pointed stones
To cover him
Where he may fall
A pall to grind his bones.

Or he one night be shown
An empty town,
In endless rain
To wander there alone:

And pass the churchyard wall
And see inside
The long-extended arms
Of the dead, stretched wide.

G.S. FRASER [1915–1980]

Crisis

My room as usual a disorder of books,
Nothing to my hand, my clothes flung on a chair,
My desk squalid and fussy with useless papers,
I had shut myself up from the clean shock of day.
I was asleep: like a criminal, without dreams.
There was nothing I desired but my own pride.

Then it seemed to me the earth opened,
I was on a green slope, an unsafe hillside,
With rocks there and rivers; there was that lady
And one man, my enemy. We three clung together
And rolled down the hill. The river whelmed,
I gripped her greedily. Then came sorrow,
She was not with me, I drowned alone:
That man mocked on the bank.

I almost awakened,
But sorrow and sleep together bind fast.
Falling far, I came to a strange city,
No one knew me, I walked in sorrow alone.
Past smoke-black brick and yellow muslin curtains,
Vainly round interminable corners,
For these streets were familiar and not familiar
(The old tenements of Glasgow and my childhood)
And I knew I would never find my own house.

Then I met myself in my dream, I said clearly,
'I am going soon, take care of yourself, find friends'.
But my own eyes looked through me, my voice said, 'Traitor!'

And I saw then
All the terrible company of the defeated,
Lost but in the courage of shapes of stone:
The stone mouths of the rigid orators,
The elbow half-lifted in a thousand club-rooms
And the steady hand on the trigger turned to stone:
Then I awoke, sweating: I came out to the window,
In the evening light saw the snow grey on the ground.
I turned to my darkening room, I saw my papers
Scattered about, my life too lately
Had been all in bits. 'My God', I said, 'there is something
Far wrong, certainly, somewhere. But with me or the world?'

How the Heart Grows Cold: 6

All that has fallen is what may befall
and that is all

and hell not ours alone is also these
befell the world and are its miseries

how could his joy reach out to hers
across a dark of unknown sufferers

across the pain
                                        the pain that does not end
when the road makes its abrupt and savage bend
or with roses and flags when the armies enter the city
or with treaties and pledges

                                        but the pain our pity
is caught up in, pity less strong than the pain

whose wheel has broken will; will break again

the torturer's will. He is broken and understands
the body's pain more than the will's desire;
how the eyes bleed, how the contorted hands
shrink from the needle, and the sex from fire.

Some who have willed this horror live,
some who have suffered this horror live,
broken wills and broken bodies.

                    Therefore in my dream
there are no living figures, therefore my love
is a seasonal echo, and there these words
have their horizon: forget, that you may forgive.

But if I sleep what wonder that I dream
or waken sweating?

                    Or that the heart,
that the poor heart, should also shrink from fire?

The Poet on His Birthday

All came to pieces in my hands,
The hesitant and the humane,
A history as flat as prose
Soiled by the salt poetic stain.

The bomb fell and the city burned
And with my palms I sifted sands
And I am paid what I have earned.

All darkness round the burning rose,
All hesitation through the dance,
All human love that habit turned
(O waters of mirage, advance!)

To lust, to hate, to glum routine
From what was ardour in the glance
Define what my restrictions mean.

All, my ingenious fancy knows:
The horror of the human scope
That turns from its fallacious hope,
All ashes, to the burning rose.

Loose these intellectual knots:
A crumbling yellow page of prose:
Murders, massacres, and plots.

Salty pillars round the plain.
Redemption through the flaming rose.
And memory the lovely stain
By which the damned his blessing knows.

KEIDRYCH RHYS [1915–1987]

Poem for a Neighbour

In the sea-marsh where I carve the harsh shallows
On the turfed rock rise a shock of willows
Stockdoves, fireflies, sea-gulls, bats from the hollows.

In the sea-marsh where outlaws starve with my Molly
On open knoll scrolls of black alder sea-holly
Instead of the screech-owl's extravagant folly.

In the sea-marsh where the buzz-hawks' talk is drover,
On sea-pulses, rag tag, lurking circles, clover,
Love-sick flicks light the nightmares of our half-drunk lover.

In the sea-marsh now springtime graves new paved with dew
On Ovid's buckler a trysting moon to Tresaith grew
Winnowed the heathcocks, magpies, cranes, sea eagles flew.

Tragic Guilt

No. I'm not an Englishman with a partisan religion.
My roots lie in another region,
Though ranged alongside yours.

But I can sense your stubbornness and your cohesion
And can even feel pride in your recent decisions
That anger reassures.

I know no love for disembodied principles, improbable tales.
The strength of the common man was always the strength of Wales,
Unashamed of her race.

May this be also England's role to bring to birth.
May she draw opposite new powers from the earth.
Huge Shakespeare has his place.

I have felt in my bones comradeship and pity,
I have seen wonders in an open door blitz city.

Amid tremendous history, new pity.

ALUN LEWIS [1915–1944]

The Sentry

I have begun to die.
For now at last I know
That there is no escape
From Night. Not any dream
Nor breathless images of sleep
Touch my bat's-eyes. I hang
Leathery-arid from the hidden roof
Of Night, and sleeplessly
I watch within Sleep's province.

I have left
The lovely bodies of the boy and girl
Deep in each other's placid arms;
And I have left
The beautiful lanes of sleep
That barefoot lovers follow to this last
Cold shore of thought I guard.
I have begun to die

And the guns' implacable silence
Is my black interim, my youth and age,
In the flower of fury, the folded poppy,
Night.

Easter at Christmas

What dark and terrible shadow is swaying in the wind?

Beautiful are thy dwellings, Lord of Hosts,
The choir-boys in white go softly singing;
The world is full of pale frustrated ghosts.

Lovers cannot reach each other;
The stars are consumed by an insane fire;
The night is red and loud; the choir-boys
Sing softly ghostly vespers of desire.

What dark and terrible shadow is swaying in the wind?

An agitator and two thieves are swaying in the wind.

Postscript: For Gweno

If I should go away,
Beloved, do not say
'He has forgotten me'.
For you abide,
A singing rib within my dreaming side;
You always stay.
And in the mad tormented valley
Where blood and hunger rally

And Death the wild beast is uncaught, untamed,
Our soul withstands the terror
And has its quiet honour
Among the glittering stars your voices named.

Goodbye

So we must say Goodbye, my darling,
And go, as lovers go, for ever;
Tonight remains, to pack and fix on labels
And make an end of lying down together.

I put a final shilling in the gas,
And watch you slip your dress beneath your knees
And lie so still I hear your rustling comb
Modulate the autumn in the trees.

And all the countless things I shall remember
Lay mummy-cloths of silence round my head;
I fill the carafe with a drink of water;
You say 'We paid a guinea for this bed',

And then, 'We'll leave some gas, a little warmth
For the next resident, and these dry flowers',
And turn your face away, afraid to speak
The big word, that Eternity is ours.

Your kisses close my eyes and yet you stare
As though God struck a child with nameless fears;
Perhaps the water glitters and discloses
Time's chalice and its limpid useless tears.

Everything we renounce except our selves;
Selfishness is the last of all to go;
Our sighs are exhalations of the earth,
Our footprints leave a track across the snow.

We made the universe to be our home,
Our nostrils took the wind to be our breath,
Our hearts are massive towers of delight,
We stride across the seven seas of death.

Yet when all's done you'll keep the emerald
I placed upon your finger in the street;
And I will keep the patches that you sewed
On my old battledress tonight, my sweet.

EMANUEL LITVINOFF [1915–2011]

To T.S. Eliot

Eminence becomes you. Now when the rock is struck
your young sardonic voice which broke on beauty
floats amid incense and speaks oracles
as though a god
utters from Russell Square and condescends
high in the solemn cathedral of the air,
his holy octaves to a million radios.

I am not one accepted in your parish.
Bleistein is my relative and I share
the protozoic slime of Shylock, a page
in *Stürmer*, and, underneath the cities,

a billet somewhat lower than the rats.
Blood in the sewers. Pieces of our flesh
float with the ordure on the Vistula.
You had a sermon but it was not this.

It would seem, then, yours is a voice
remote, singing another river
and the gilded wreck of princes only
for Time's ruin. It is hard to kneel
when knees are stiff.

But London Semite Russian Pale, you will say
Heaven is not in our voices.
The accent, I confess, is merely human,
speaking of passion with a small letter
and, crying widow, mourning not the Church
but a woman staring the sexless sea
for no ship's return,
and no fruit singing in the orchards.

Yet walking with Cohen when the sun exploded
and darkness choked our nostrils,
and the smoke drifting over Treblinka
reeked of the smouldering ashes of children,
I thought what an angry poem
you would have made of it, given the pity.

But your eye is a telescope
scanning the circuit of stars
for Good-Good and Evil Absolute,
and, at luncheon, turns fastidiously from fleshy
noses to contemplation of the knife
twisting among the entrails of spaghetti.

So shall I say it is not eminence chills
but the snigger from behind the covers of history?
Let your words
tread lightly on this earth of Europe
lest my people's bones protest.

SYDNEY GOODSIR SMITH [1915–1975]

Armageddon in Albyn: II: The Mither's Lament

Whit care I for the leagues o sand,
The prisoners and the gear they've won?
Ma darlin liggs amang the dunes
Wi mony a mither's son.

Doutless he deed for Scotland's life;
Doutless the statesmaen dinna lee;
But och tis sair begrutten pride
An wersh the wine o victorie!

ROLAND MATHIAS [1915–2007]

The Bearers

Wet in the field,
A dull rook preaching
To congregated hecklers in the trees,
And there, behind the text from Maccabees,
Red warfare reaching
Into this ground, in upturned blood revealed.

Yet I am home
With handgrip, knowing
Something there is that turns me to the hills,
Some bowel-moving look about me tills
The body going
To growth. I am turned bonewards in this loam.

And when I go,
A burden and bearing,
O long the labour the dark Beacons make
Cloudwise across the south, and me they take
Covertly faring,
An Eginhard over the unfallen snow.

PATRICK LEIGH FERMOR [1915–2011]

from *Greek Archipelagoes*

Ἐν ἀρχῇ ἦν ὁ λόγος
From the north
The autumn wind carries the storks over Patmos
From Kiev and Bukovina, Rila and the Euxine,
Mystra and Athos and the hanging Meteora,
Stretching their necks for Sinai. The slow armada
Tangles the passage of the Word of God:
A load of plumed and shifting fruit
Bends the branches of the only tree.

The Word of God split the rocks here
And built this battlemented monastery
On rocks that are Magians cast down and turned to stone,
To hide the Word, the leisure of the monks
From scimitars of the corsairs, a stone casket
For treasure of Constantinople and the Russias,
Mitres and flasks and chrysobuls and scrolls,
Gifts of half-legendary voivodes, and the crosiers
Of bishops who became saints.
(Foreheads of parchment seen in silver coffins,
Palimpsests where the flourishes of mortality are faded
Under the calligraphy of beatitude.)

The wind in the soaking darkness winds
Through rocks and roofs, lifting the unwilling wing
Of huddling storks.
Thunder explodes, and the shuddering apocalypse
Of lightning bares the shapes of cupolas
The mountain-side and rain-logged wings
And tethered caïques that rear like frightened horses.

FRANCIS BERRY [1915–2006]

Farvel

'Listen,
Oswald, Olaf, or Olsen:

Wrily twisting at the mouth he died,
Orion sprawling in the eastern sky.

The Winged and Swarthy hurried to his side
With shadows wrapt and hooded him
And shouldered him and fled.

Fled with the whining of the wind,
Riding with the hollow screaming of the blore
And the black waves there below.

Nu, ved Norden!
Cliff-spumed,
(and the black waves there below),
Very vast and nocturne shored.

Dod! ved Norden
Where distant pennons dimly flutter

For he is dead.
Han? Dod'.

PATRICK ANDERSON [1915–1979]

Excitement

Excitement
blesses the objects. Form can give
security. One hides in the attractive
sense of an island. But tonight
by the oil lamp in the parlour
or changing my shoes on the cold linoleum
by the light of a candle, running out on the sand,
or turning into the sea-dark at the doorway,
vague, warm, the moth in the wind
damp on the privet and fuchsia,
the honeysuckle swung with a tendril
and the ivy clipped to the rock and the heather
wired to its peaty soil,
I shall be ashamed of alliteration
and the obvious delight. I shall be ashamed
of rootless sensuality that pumps
the blood-red flower and impacts the stone,
for the poem behind the poem is inconsolable.
I shall want to cry with my own voice:
'I have come back. It is after ten years.
How does one learn to live?' and the question,
hidden behind the question, once again,
will rise in its unconscionable boyhood
to be the gunman of another twilight.

DORIAN COOKE [1916–2005]

Gethsemane Poem

Broken the falling hour cropped in the stormed heel,
And blinds no winter there, sack-print of legend
Nor the lank-death fathom bruised weather-grief
With tied-and-dungeon tongue.

Thick emblem to the danger's end, to the weal
And scarecrow in the curse: five wounds and pierce
The mirror's veins through the black hill's pitchfork
And foul deluge in the prong.

Struck fire from the danger's deed, it was the blood
Speaks brutal to the wine, all crumpled and dumb
And the five worlds' famine heave carrion shine
Or the dark man filter stone.

Never the forced murder for the fighting mud,
I listen down the agony and the cracked war
And number heavens in the hell-riven man
From rape and the firework clown.

I burrowed forged in the pattern of this flood,
And on each bitter rampart burn the twin world
In sap, drowning the bright Word one sleep down
Who grows where flesh is sown.

To Wendy

I call this daybreak for my hands have pressed the Earth
And the lighted wonder of its workaday sorrow.
Listen, darling, to the world-beats in that hour when,
Dying like a death-star in its birth, with hunger and snow
We lived and lay like one world dead. It was daybreak in the North.

More than my darkness a cold breath and spawn had lined
The shrieking myth with a symphony of madness.
Then swung from the throttled map and fang soft fury
Like a seed, token to fire and foul the deadness:
And across a crippled stranger fell the full-lipped whirlwind.

What ways, what fumbled sunstroke lead from flood to echo?
This handiwork of days recalls a fire and death.
Our joy, your paradox, my life are stronger than
The scream that wrings the triple sunset from your mouth.
Then rest, muttered world! words heave and rinse the deeds they blow.

Poem in Memory of Theodora Hendry
(As a letter to J.F.H.)

They told me she was dead.
I hear the far, sharp turmoil turn to flesh,
And the flesh break up into constituent seed.
I hear the seed burning into riper ash.

Across the two years' rubble and slow dusks
I know your days, and how all your nights turn round
Like a wheel in a flood. And a wheel of beaten husks
Has blown to fire and scorched the harvested land.

I would look on, but my eyes must strike the blind
And furious ways – that fever-eating waste
Of wide, unquenchable seas that pack their storms
Between me and that death. These are the first
To fall. The last is mortal, bearing the dragon's arms.

They told me she had died.
O, let me shake awake the mortal storm,
The frozen berries, the white
Still drops of light.
Dreams fester like a drug-polluted mud,
And thorns are quenched in an unhallowed dream.
So let me beat awake the visions I have grown,
Death in the soil of the marrow,
The bone that gives to bone
A life that lives tomorrow.
By faith a man must creep
Out of the cisterns of cold sleep.

The dead lie deep. No ancient hymn
Can cramp their damp hearth or unfold
Their heart's blood in a web of gold.
Surely nerve and limb
Must halt when a man is alone in his anger.
But the dead are forever old,
And have no limbs that linger.

Break up! I see how the map
Between us stirs in its darkness. Like a railway track
Hunger and madness twist on the page and stop
Where the dead rot frozen in their sweat. Back,
Ring back across the aching seas
Five million footfalls. No wind can make
This clapper swing. No, it is not the time to remember these.

I summon again
That death. I summon to the narrow, unwilling evening
The reprieve of her laughter, and her unbroken eyes. Soon
The ways must close, their bitter sentries screaming
To the North and the South. Yet now she would speak
And suffer, she would bustle among books and men.
Those are not her lips that break
This distance. No, she is a faceless shroud
Of memories and dissolving bones;
And to her shut, bleak bed
No one comes to knock upon the stones.

Tides move to battle – parable or flame.
The patchwork of huge faith
Died too; and we are outlaws
Watching from the last, live room.
But her body only shows
The miracle of the forgiving earth.

A Soldier, Dying of Wounds, Speaks to me on May 9th, 1945

You will remain. Do not hope much
From the husks of heavy archives;
Their tongues bark dusty lies that touch
Your footway. The enemy has lives
Still and a long language. You will clutch
Many times there, and you will flicker
Like a lamp in the wind. Your mark
Is known, for it does not beat quicker
Than an old cradle. Search the dark
For signs, and the far light
For footprints from the night.

Do not dream much in the waiting years,
Nor guess an incredible way
Up mountain clouds or down damp stairs
Through the illiterate dark. Each day
The ambush is armed against your heirs,
Levies are laid on living and dying.
I am among those who have died;
All our deaths, like a hurt child crying,
Are only a by-work. The wind-tide,
Water-call, fall of rain,
Are for those who remain.

from *Autumn to Summer Sequence*

The beginning green again, ending a story;
The important earth; seedlings of a sorrow to come:
Such news is modified in human fury,
As aliens are in a concentration camp.
It's nesting time in the unswept slums of glory.
Heaven's stairs are steep, that the carrion have to climb.

Now while the sun's long faces curl and climb
Into summer again, a same storm story
Sends birds from the ends of the seas to encamp
In the trees or the churchyard pump; and a same sour fury
Will later expel them; but no one, now they have come,
Will repel them. Cinders of sun must make red glory

In flowers and the skins of fruit out of cold green glory
Which is just beginning to grow. The rough, slow climb
Out of winter is told as an innumerable story
With all the expected endings; some that will come

Too soon and some too late, – all like a hopeless fury
Scratching for coins on the site of a Roman camp.

I have been inmate in several kinds of camp;
And I remember how at times dark spots of glory
Would dance on the bright sheets of my dreams and become
Parts of oblivion, like characters in a long story
Lost before it has been told; no gold ghosts climb
Into time there, ironclad busybodies, nor the fury

Of frost and flesh: this soft thaw into the fury
Of waking (like the first bugle-note that silvers half the camp)
Puts an end to a whole day's lives, to an hour and a glory
Of multitudinous man. So I have tried to climb
To the halfway house between the beginning and the story
Of summer; and somewhere, with the times behind and to come

In their special relation, I know that I must come
To an utter situation, carrying my gifts of fury
In a bundle on my back. But in the slithery climb
Over time how many rumours will fall? What glory
Goes on, with a world that has shrunk like a camp
Where hunger, hangmen and disease do the work of the story?

Summers are an anonymous story, for they always come
With their face-fury blank and go like a broken transit camp
For refugees. Glory is a mountain that beginners climb.

DAVID GASCOYNE [1916–2001]

Zero: September, 1939

Who can by now not hear
The hollow and annihilating roar
Of final disillusion; or not know
How our condition is uncertain and obscure
And difficult to bear? Yet through
The blackness of his dungeon there still peer
Man's eyes, unmoving, lit by their desire
To see *the worst*, and yet not die
Of their lucid despair
But in such vision persevere
Through time into Eternity.
For this is Zero-hour
When the most penetrating gaze can see
Only the Void, the emptier than air,
The incoherent *Nada* of the seer:
Who blind is yet not blind, being aware
Of the Negation's double mystery!

Tomb of what was, womb of what is to be.

A Wartime Dawn

Dulled by the slow glare of the yellow bulb;
As far from sleep still as at any hour
Since distant midnight; with a hollow skull
In which white vapours seem to reel
Among limp muddles of old thought; till eyes
Collapse into themselves like clams in mud...
Hand paws the wall to reach the chilly switch;

Then nerve-shot darkness gradually shakes
Throughout the room. *Lie still…* Limbs twitch;
Relapse to immobility's faint ache. And time
A while relaxes; space turns wholly black.

But deep in the velvet crater of the ear
A chip of sound abruptly irritates.
A second, a third chirp; and then another far
Emphatic trill and chirrup shrills in answer; notes
From all directions round pluck at the strings
Of hearing with frail finely-sharpened claws.
And in an instant, every wakened bird
Across surrounding miles of air
Outside, is sowing like a scintillating sand
Its throat's incessantly replenished store
Of tuneless singsong, timeless, aimless, blind.

Draw now with prickling hand the curtains back;
Unpin the blackout-cloth; let in
Grim crack-of-dawn's first glimmer through the glass.
All's yet half-sunk in Yesterday's stale death,
Obscurely still beneath a moist-tinged blank
Sky like the inside of a deaf mute's mouth…
Nearest within the window's sight, ash-pale
Against a cinder-coloured wall, the white
Pear-blossom hovers like a stare; rain-wet
The further housetops weakly shine; and there,
Beyond, hangs flaccidly a lone barrage-balloon.

An incommunicable desolation weighs
Like depths of stagnant water on this brink of day. –
Long meditation without thought. – Until a breeze
From some pure Nowhere straying, stirs
A pang of poignant odour from the earth, an unheard sigh

Pregnant with sap's sweet tang and raw soil's fine
Aroma, smell of stone, and acrid breath
Of gravel puddles. While the brooding green
Of nearby gardens' grass and trees, and quiet flat
Blue leaves, the distant lilac mirages, are made
Clear by increasing daylight, and intensified.

Now head sinks into pillows in retreat
Before this morning's hovering advance;
(Behind loose lids, in sleep's warm porch, half hears
White hollow clink of bottles, – dragging crunch
Of milk-cart wheels, – and presently a snatch
Of windy whistling as the newsboy's bike winds near,
Distributing to neighbours' peaceful steps
Reports of last night's battles;) at last sleeps.
While early guns on Norway's bitter coast
Where faceless troops are landing, renew fire:
And one more day of War starts everywhere.

P.K. PAGE [1916–2010]

Death

So this was death –
the hummingbird's soft throat
bound in a dark and crimson coat
of blood.
This flood
of feeling in her heart
was the essential part
of life.
The strife

of living was a little thing beside
the sobbing, throbbing eventide
of breath.

Earthquake

Look at the sky, she said
as the earth quaked
and others were taking cover.
You might see God
in the brief irregular shape
framed by the falling hotels
with their ferns hurtling.
In the space between
the still standing church
and the teetering Five and Ten
he might be seen
as small and bright as a straight pin
narrowly smiling.
This is the kind of time
He might appear to be near
shining and clear.
Look at the sky, she said,
but brimful brick
filled in a twinkling
the dwindling opening
and sky came tumbling.

from *If It Were You*

If it were you, say, you
who scanning the personal map one day knew
your sharp eyes water and grow colour-blind,
unable to distinguish green from blue
and everything terribly run together as if rain
had smudged the markings on the paper –
a child's painting after a storm –
and the broad avenue erased,
the landmarks gone;
and you, bewildered – not me this time and not
the cold unfriendly neighbour or the face in the news –
who walked a blind circle in a personal place;

and if you became lost, say, on the lawn,
unable to distinguish left from right
and that strange longitude that divides the body
sharply in half – that line that separates
so that one hand could never be the other –
dissolved and both your hands were one,
then in the garden though birds went on with their singing
and on the ground
flowers wrote their signatures in coloured ink –
would you call help like a woman assaulted,
cry to be found?

[…]

Would you call Ariel, Ariel, in the garden,
in a dream within a dream be Orpheus
and for a certain minute take a step
delicately across the grass?

If so, there would be no answer or reply
and not one coming forward from the leaves.
No bird nor beast with a challenging look
or friendly.
Simply nothing but you and the green garden,
you and the garden.

[…]

Might you not, if it were you,
bewildered, broken,
slash your own wrists, commit
an untidy murder in the leafy lane
and scar the delicate air with your cries or sit
weeping, weeping in the public square
your flimsy butterfly fingers in your hair
your face destroyed by rain?

If it were you, the person you call 'I',
the one you loved and worked for,
the most high
now become Ishmael,
might you not
grow phobias about calendars and clocks,
stare at your face in the mirror, not knowing it
and feel an identity with idiots and dogs
as all the exquisite unborns of your dreams
deserted you to snigger behind their hands?

THOMAS BLACKBURN [1916–1977]

Hospital for Defectives

By your unnumbered charities
A miracle disclose,
Lord of the Images, whose love
The eyelid and the rose
Takes for a language, and today
Tell to me what is said
By these men in a turnip field
And their unleavened bread.

For all things seem to figure out
The stirrings of your heart,
And two men pick the turnips up
And two men pull the cart;
And yet between the four of them
No word is ever said
Because the yeast was not put in
Which makes the human bread.
But three men stare on vacancy
And one man strokes his knees;
What is the meaning to be found
In such dark vowels as these?

Lord of the images, whose love
The eyelid and the rose
Takes for a metaphor, today
Beneath the warder's blows,
The unleavened man did not cry out
Or turn his face away;
Through such men in a turnip field
What is it that you say?

PHILIP O'CONNOR [1916–1998]

The Baby

The baby should have oranges, which would run through him
nourishingly
He would then make more noise,
we would wash him, he would shine like silver spoons.

Perhaps he is ill
from the scowling windows. They should be
clear like air to let sun through.

This is impossible. Bag
after bag of soft
dirt
could be collected out of London air.

He should breathe, live,
wave his arms well and
show extremely white teeth
amongst pleasant smells
and moving currents
of fresh air. This is impossible. He will mumble,
whine, clamouringly cry. Go white
like bacon-fat,
smell like a urinal,
play with dirt, gobble cheap food,
have crooked legs and too-staring eyes,
fall easily and hit viciously, grin like a wolf
and leap for food,
suspiciously cater for himself. This is inevitable.

JACK CLEMO [1916–1994]

Clay-Land Moods: I

There squats amid these pyramids
The Sphinx-mood of a Deity,
Unfelt until He bids
Sandstorms awaken and the choking dust
Drive me across the moors of barren trust.
Then I perceive the aloof grey shape, the scorn,
Quiet veiled cruelty of the watching eyes:
The grim mysterious Will all help denies.
The feet press out until my roots are torn,
Caught by the mauling claws. In silence He
Smothers and tortures me.

Here on the sharp clay-tip there broods
Olympian thunder, bold and swift,
Fiercest of all God's moods.
One flash therefrom and peaks of vision seethe
With hostile potency: while wrathful vapours writhe
I creep down rain-grooves, cravenly slink to hide
In caves of the pit, and bruised with panic prayer
Unknown to Mammon's sober workmen there,
I wait till lightnings, thunder-rasps have died
And God allows his terror-mood to lift
From off the senseless rift.

There is a certain mystic hour
When pyramid and clay-tip grow
Alive with darker power;
A mood unknown to Nature, a mortal mood
Caught up into His Godhead: taste of blood,
Anguish that makes each tip-frame a gibbet, bared

Until I feel on each the swing of my hand, a pale
Ghost-self of primal guilt that drives the nail.
And the Sphinx-mood is mercy, Olympus tame compared
With my deserts. Then I begin to know
Why I am tested so.

Epilogue: Priest Out of Bondage

I

Dark, mutinous land: I shared
Its moods through my dead youth, but I am spared
To wake and live and know it a husk and tetter
Which faith and sunrise peel from my soul.
I slip with every other fetter
The Cornish bond, for I must be whole
Within the eternal Moment, and have no root
In soil or race, in the annals
Of the Celt, or in the dubious channels
Whence idiosyncrasies and tensions shoot.

II

I rise, no longer dark,
No longer mutinous, and embark
On the journey outward, the escape
To air that is rid of superstition, to a pulse
That draws no heavy blood from the obscure
Cycles of savagery, the historic shape
Of atavism. I shed the lure
Of a dim mother-breast I have outgrown,
And while the Moment's fierce hot joys convulse
My heart I take the irrevocable step beyond

Loyalty to this dead land: no longer bone
Of my bone is its granite, nor flesh
Of my flesh its clay:
The bright blade of the Word severs the barbarous bond.

III

Christ calls from the tarred road and I must go,
Not as an exile, no,
Nor as one deprived, but as one
Moving to fulfilment, moving home
Out of the ancestral mesh,
Out of the bitter moorlands where my tears
Fell on the sullen bramble and the dun
Rock of the derelict years.
Heir of the Moment and the electing Way
Whence all my treasures come,
I tread in the newness of truth
Where dawn-flushed pylons trample the uncouth
Spells of the tribal night. And this dead land
Which bore and moulded me for a fate
Sour as its soil and hard with its hate
Smoulders and glowers behind the plucked brand
It will never regain or understand.

TERENCE TILLER [1916–1987]

The word is all: the bell and the wind-bird

The word is all: the bell and the wind-bird
clamour and sway so high, the hunted climber
dreams his voice, the lonely moss, his limbs,
are haters in darkness and the dirk in the heather.

The word is nothing: wrath in the unreal storm
eats but the air, terrifies with lights;
ghosts but menace; man soon forgets
the falling of the tower, and the tree-felling.

The only answer lances towards the unknown:
fear in the eyes, the wisdom of a seer
forcing true gods through imagined sources;
hell, in the dreaming heart, heard in the bell.

The Islanders

Crouched in the womb I learned this fear:
the subtle streams that fed me moved
in darkness, and my fish's ear
took dimly from the outer air
nothing I knew or loved.

Then between lifted thighs I broke
into a level bed of weeping; found
strong to the pouring air as rock,
and grimly rooted like the oak,
the inevitable round.

A farthing frond of beauty hid
the weevil in my green delight;
but round my pillow came the dead,
and the unborn were garmented
in guttering wicks by night.

Then to that other darkness came
behind my lidded eyes, the blood
that beat around me in the womb;
under my fingers crept the worm
of bonds and solitude.

Now the great bones of ancient things
lie foundered on the rotting beach;
the fear of death betrays our tongues;
our beds are full of whisperings:
blind, we turn each to each.

We lift involuntary hands
out of our separate dream; but still
the goblin like a gantry stands
with arms forbidding, and unwinds
the fibres of the soul.

Lights wander between us, and we crouch
while inaccessible pain and love
fasten upon the external touch:
silent around us, the worlds watch
our useless fear of death and life.

JULIAN ORDE [1917–1974]

The Awaiting Adventure

Dear stranger, the mule is loaded, let us start.
A tune of trees is written across the hill,
And the sky is high, today, and nothing is still,
But I feel banners thudding against a wind,
A cave of wings rushing over the ground,
And the leaping day calling me into love.

The expert from the city tunes the trees
In far snowfields of sleep we may not cross;
The revolving lighthouse is adrift and lost –
But oh! I am awake and running down
The yellow slopes of my tomorrow's hopes!

There is about us more than a man's mind,
More than a ship's huge voyaging and end
Or the whole brass music of a gallant day.
The jet of life has sprung its ecstasy:
I am in love with greater than I am,
And share the way of stone and star and lamb,
And even the central, liquid rock moves in me.

Always, stranger, let us be setting out,
With home not left but in ourselves always.
The eager fabulist of holy orders
Will log our journey for us in the night,
And – if we let him – ride ahead and praise.

The hierarchy of mountains does not speak,
But the cold flowers, with a different life,
And in a different time, create and die,

Familiar with the deathless walls of ice;
Not seeing their fathers' shape against the sky.

Stranger, met at last, this great beginning
Shall swing us through all times and all planes;
Though we but walk, are little, and have names,
Our history is in us and we in history.

The Upward Rain

Dropped, let fall with a sigh, the clouds have released rain;
The brown earth hisses and swarms up the silver branches,
Green climbs to the sky till the clouds are swelling with flowers.
Splashed come the fruit and the bees and the waves of the tree;
Flashing wet metal, there is sudden arrival of dragonflies,
Held in the air by their rigid and quivering wings like church windows.
Such a meeting of water and lovers of water I see!
Such communion of flower and cloud and the waves of the tree!

The Lonely Company

No explanation blew a wider gate
Than finding how closely carried early and late
In what I must call the heart or breast
Are the bright figures of the just,
Those who, since the first splash of a stone,
Now, and tomorrow, are the best of us.

Born under Capricorn to be
Most criminal yet also the most free,
Who, after the mind takes them down
Into the bitter town,

Return with some weeping,
Gone soft with the gentleness of the home-coming;
The most afraid and best prepared for death
And the day of wrath.

They do not come with bombs
Yet are made unwelcome.
Above the sad-frocked and the flicker-eyed
They spike like stars.
I leave it to them, not nuns, to say my prayers,
And since this gate blew wide
Know we shall never be separated
For where they are there the heart goes along.
They are the company I would choose to die among.

The Changing Wind

Past my window runs a tree,
All the leaves are in my room,
A shiver of water passes over.
There is no stillness ever again.

I saw the table break in three,
I saw the walls cascading down,
I saw the hard hair of my lover
Drift out upon the flowing green.
I saw the clove dark enemy
Stare from the bed where I had lain,
I saw my face in hers to be.
There is no stillness ever again.

Sun and wind had come for me –
What is my house but a flight of wings?
A flight of leaves, a flutter of rain,
A sidelong slipping of light in rings?

And now a scream possesses me –
Too high to hear, yet can I hear it;
And now transfixed upon a pain,
Too thin to feel yet must I bear it –
This scream, this pain, they are not mine,
Water and air is all I am,
A tree has shaken the staircase down –
Then what has rustled and entered in?

I knew the other ones had come.
I knew my heart was theirs to claim.
I felt the millions in my room.
There is no being alone again.

from *Conjurors*

Something has so altered in the night,
    Surely the wind changed to make this?
        The racking caterpillar gone
        And a pale nymph lightly borne
Under the old thread. Might
    It be a ghost? The mask on its face
    Has a beak of gold. It is like a little fish!

It is like a waxen fish
    Filled with green leaves
        With a veiny hint
        Of two wings' imprint,

With a waist, with a twitch-
ing tail, with a sheaf
Of yellow dots. It is hooded like a witch.

It has come among us hooded
And it has no bones!
It cannot walk
It wears a long cloak
But is also naked;
It is the skin round albumen,
The caul, the bag about the yolk.

[…]

Fourteen days, and then a crack!
A skull-grey face with tendril-coiled
Antennae; wet
Wings, in folds yet
Of greenish gold with spots of black,
And a grey fur back, walk like a child
Unbalancedly into the world.

The involutions of her early wings
Invite a finger's cruelty
To know the damp
Place where she once dwelt,
Or to deface and itself win
From each cold hollow, guiltily,
Some of the dews and dustings of her beauty.

She walks like a boat on the beach
Dragging her drying sails,
While the last
Memory of her past

Shakes from her tail: a bead
Of amber dew, unnoticed as the shell
That husked and housed her in its brittle walls.

Climber of curtains, long she'll not hang there;
Taut are her wings and head-dress.
She will feed on sweet
Slippets but will never eat.
She will find her answering angel in the air.
She will not lay her eggs upon nasturtiums' crease
And will not remember the taste of the leaf.

Suddenly she is soundlessly flapping across the broad
Floor of the air without a trial;
The sun takes her
Across to the blue buddleia.
Out of her depths in air she is not afraid.
When she reaches the tree she finds it full
Of her own shapes and becomes indistinguishable.

CHARLES CAUSLEY [1917–2003]

For an Ex-Far East Prisoner of War

I am that man with helmet made of thorn
Who wandered naked in the desert place,
Wept, with the sweating sky, that I was born
And wore disaster in my winter face.

I am that man who asked no hate, nor pity.
I am that man, five-wounded, on the tree.
I am that man, walking his native city,
Hears his dead comrade cry, *Remember me!*

I am that man whose brow with blood was wet,
Returned, as Lazarus, from the dead to live.
I am that man, long counselled to forget,
Facing a fearful victory, to forgive:

And seizing these two words, with the sharp sun
Beat them, like sword and ploughshare, into one.

D.S. SAVAGE [1917–2007]

Landscape

There where the river shrank past shack and shelter
I dug the iron earth and planted iron
for mutilated trees to drip all winter
out of the itching of the dangerous sun.

I planted dragonteeth: and men of metal
armoured with anger climbed from the sullen ground
aching with pain to murder the maternal
and spill the running wax with which they groaned.

And where they paced the torn ramshackle circle
of grief and sin the crippled shells of pain
rose from the bed of sorrow with a manacle
of splintered bone to ring the bursting sun.

There where the gasdrums hoisted through the city
I hacked a corpse of grass and fed with death
the mouth of seaweed in a ghastly pity,
and drove my martyred men again to death.

Confession

You have said, for certain
To be true, to be good
Words must be written
In the heart's blood.

I have tried, I have tried,
I have laboured and toiled

Till the ink dried
Or the blood cooled.

I know that blood is bitter,
That ink tastes sour,
The hand runs better
When the heart is sure.

I walk among men
With my labour and pain,
Blood on the pen,
Ink in the vein.

Separation

All day I have been completely alone, and now the night
Descends, swathing in shadow and swaddling all,
And all but a smother and blur is bandaged from sight,
Blots and blotches of shadow clotting on ceiling and wall.

I lift the glass chimney and light the oil-lamp's wick,
The quick lick of the flame flickers, and shadows distend,
The elongations of fingers sprawl on the wall, and the tick
Of the tin clock in the silence and the tick of my pulse contend.

In this prolongation of solitude, I am estranged
Even from myself, in you; in your absence I dwindle apart
In a ghostly attenuation of feeling, till all my deranged
Consciousness aches in the void for the physical thud of your heart.

ROBERT CONQUEST [1917–2015]

Guided Missiles Experimental Range

Soft sounds and odours brim up through the night
A wealth below the level of the eye;
Out of a black, an almost violet sky
Abundance flowers into points of light.

Till from the south-west, as their low scream mars
And halts this warm hypnosis of the dark,
Three black automata cut swift and stark,
Shaped clearly by the backward flow of stars.

Stronger than lives, by empty purpose blinded,
The only thought their circuits can endure is
The target-hunting rigour of their flight;

And by that loveless haste I am reminded
Of Aeschylus' description of the Furies:
'O barren daughters of the fruitful night'.

NICHOLAS MOORE [1918–1986]

from *The Dog's Days (For Priscilla)*

Now iron courage touches every heart,
The coward is made whole. The crooked road
Of centuries lies straightened in the dust,
A shining moonlit way for us to tread,
Dreading no more, happy to earn our fate:
We go, we go, fiercely because we must.

The statesmen we have dreaded are our heroes,
The laws we strove against our soundest hope,
The murderer with his velvet axe has honour
Now that death stands at ease on every lip:
No more than motes now all our private sorrows:
Love has no finery left here upon her.

Bomb for bomb, strength for strength, anger for
Anger, we must heap hate on our foes,
Careful now of the peaceful man, of our neighbour,
Suspicious of his unknown, searching eyes:
For who can search for peace within a war,
And not destroy our courage in his labour?

Now iron courage, now the dauntless heart.
The coward must be whole, the crooked straight.
We must forget the long-gone centuries,
We must forget our private love and hate;
Nor we are wise, whom only love can hurt,
Who have no dreams behind our hating eyes.

Two Acrobats With a Hare

I

Today they stand, two known figures in a ritual
No longer known, young man and young woman
            Hand in hand.

Their eyes are round as moons, but black,
Move to each other and back, in a love
            Hard to prove

But apparent. It is the way they move.
It is this way that is love; the movement
            Of what they are.

And next time will be the same,
And the next time, and we never will
            Finish the dream.

For it is as symbols that they stand, star and star,
Bright and hopeful, the young as they are.

II

The hare leaps, as the spirit moves
Between the two, and their loves
Compose themselves to a point
Like a star and grow faint.
They watch the hare in the moon, and the face
Of the moon-goddess brilliant in its place,
And in the mirror of their error
They see how strong they are, and all their terror.
But it is a terror of reason, seasonable,

And, though they fear, they are not incapable.
They do not worship idols or ideals,
But hold on to what is real:
That the real may finally exorcise their fear
And each leap to the other as lightly as a hare.

Citadel of Despised Populations

The nerves contend against the elements.
The nerves taste quinces in the watered winds,
Upon the skin taste effluence of hairs.
The tower of Judas is no thought of theirs,
No more than they would think of womanly
Diversions. To be cried is not to cry.
Above each city floats a selfless sky.

To touch the senses it is not enough
To teach treasons. Desire is of despised
Influences. Settle your affair
With the appropriate formulas, and there
Naked she stands, a handsome figurine
Of short perfections. Nerves acclaim her eye,
But carve her limbs to make a blasphemy.

Sufficient to the snake is the gazelle,
Whereof and by the right. Wriggle of riddles
Never taught handsome Judas to be free.
Nerves scented honey in the fallen tree,
The self composed to die upon a pole.
The axe is fallen in the bloodless wine,
The citadel so comforted, with rhyme.

Two Political Poems: 2: The Natural Form

The illiterate and lonely
Who earlier combined
Against necessity only,
The blind who were not blind

Enough for complete deception,
And from their certain need
Outlined the future's action,
Planted there like a seed

In the English earth a plant
That would flower in a new society.
Thus from this ancient want
Grows our imagined city,

Brilliant with light for all
And Time with its stone arm
Is powerless to appal
The future's natural form.

Breath

Impotent in the face of Death;
Impotent, perhaps, in the face of life;
Your loss cuts through me like a knife:
Gone, gone, in the act of taking breath.

For without breath, we are nothing, cold as stone.
I am cold too. Still breathing, but alone
Yet, if you were alive, I know you would have me go on

The way I am going, past the forlorn and hopeless,
Writing, writing and making whatever I can of new happiness:

You were always generous towards such success.

W.S. GRAHAM [1918–1986]

The Narrator

I am the hawk-heart braced in the epic's hero
Hollow and lit in a single follyless zone
Twinned with a dawn and a dark.
Graceless in gardens I hear my unvisited care
Squawk back at the sculptured cuckoo's nursery rhyme
Chimed in the dandelion tower.
Eyelashed and petald alone in the shepherd season
I walk heaved high from the earth confessing the voice
That runs ever over the hour
Confessing the death without space for the laying of dead
The rudder and rocket stem and the murder swerve
At the tender right-wrong heart.

The hiccuping hero the narrator lindenward
Reels at the waltz with diaphanous water fronds
Telling his ribbed in vanity.
I worship a skylift of Narnain blaeberry globed
Priest-like sealed in a tensile sac in a nerve
In the vein-geared bubble of vision.
While whisper the tethered anemones under the grave
And the narrative sprouts from the bone-sweet skull
Telling a blossom to its bulb
And spins in a hollow of sound in the emerald dome

Tinctured vermilion and told in the glacier heart
That trades the unmapped spell along the blood.

The raven at larchtime dwarfed in the calyxed chronicle
In my head's helmet weathers no wheeling sky.
The banished bird spins no horizon.
Yet my eye webs the word. History in a bowl
Spreads out a firth for ptarmigan and the pedlar's moth
And anarchy within a cage.
Who knows the rose or quotes her holy somersaults
Preached from a dangled spinner on a maypole thread.
What summer eyes perched deep within a dream
Could bring the god the child and the rose to speak.
What tongue like a stamen stemmed on a kiss or a grave
Is yet enchanted into form.

Over the Apparatus of the Spring is Drawn

Over the apparatus of the spring is drawn
A constructed festival of pulleys from sky.
A dormouse swindled from numbers into wisdom
Trades truth with bluebells. The result unknown
Fades in the sandy beetle-song that martyrs hear
Who longingly for violetcells prospect the meads.

As luck would testify, the trend for logic's sake
Takes place on pleasant landscapes within graves
That flesh, the sun's minister, in jealous agonies
Seeks out in choral vagaries with bird and blood.
Those funnels of fever (but melody to gales)
Tenant the spiral answer of a scarecrow daisy.

The country crimes are doctrines on the grass
Preaching a book of veins. The answer is order.
A derrick in flower swings evening values in
And wildernight or garden day frames government
For thieves in a prison of guilt. Birches erect
The ephemeral mechanism of welcoming.
And Spring conquests the law in a cuckoo's school.

This Fond Event My Origin Knows Well

This fond event my origin knows well
How this nativity the young twig's editor
Sees progress down
At a bone-depth bore the grave's gravel
And squabble for April's blessing.

My heart is headhung on a peartree girl
Whirled from the season's pollen flume.
The maiden fiddle
Fresh from the dogslept dawn fanfares the flesh
That crushed a clover fleece and a wing's wall.

Being bound all sworn ways when fable in flood
Treads on the holy heel, to lay out green
The earthy eyes
That tread the iris-cobbled park of wonders
I pluck a lexicon of May-locked riddles.

This I can better love than tell in virgins
How this philosophy the mind's ambition
Sees parliament down
At a bone-depth bore the grave's gravel
And squabble for April's blessing.

Listen. Put on Morning

Listen. Put on morning.
Waken into falling light.
A man's imagining
Suddenly may inherit
The handclapping centuries
Of his one minute on earth.
And hear the virgin juries
Talk with his own breath
To the corner boys of his street.
And hear the Black Maria
Searching the town at night.
And hear the playropes caa
The sister Mary in.
And hear Willie and Davie
Among bracken of Narnain
Sing in a mist heavy
With myrtle and listeners.
And hear the higher town
Weep a petition of fears
At the poorhouse close upon
The public heartbeat.
And hear the children tig
And run with my own feet
Into the netting drag
Of a suiciding principle.
Listen. Put on lightbreak.
Waken into miracle.
The audience lies awake
Under the tenements
Under the sugar docks
Under the printed moments.
The centuries turn their locks

And open under the hill
Their inherited books and doors
All gathered to distil
Like happy berry pickers
One voice to talk to us.
Yes listen. It carries away
The second and the years
Till the heart's in a jacket of snow
And the head's in a helmet of white
And the song sleeps to be wakened
By the morning ear bright.
Listen. Put on morning.
Waken into falling light.

JOHN HEATH-STUBBS [1918–2006]

Two Men in Armour

Stark by the Eastern gate
Stand the two iron men
Full-throated singing

As when before-dawn darkness
Lolls on the Earth, the impossible season
Of flesh subsided or nerves drawn tighter,
The fire-hackled, blood-wattled, needle-spurred cock
Stretches his wings through the blackness, proclaims,

The iron hand is on your shoulder
The iron hand is on your head.

When pickpocket water strips the flesh
Green-fingered, lurching the drowned limbs, choking
The pale throat, drums on the bursting eyes;
And rolls and rolls where monstrous things go by,
All selfhood murdered, twitched beneath that tide –

(The iron hand is in your hand)
– When fire filches the proud heart from you, faggoting
Your bones for kindling – oh my Prince
Let music go up then, let praise go up
Like shepherd's fluting on the lonely hills.

Till Love construe the cryptic iron faces.

The Divided Ways: In Memory of Sidney Keyes

He has gone down into the dark cellar
To talk with the bright-faced Spirit with silver hair;
But I shall never know what word was spoken there.

My friend is out of earshot. Our ways divided
Before we even knew we had missed each other.
For he advanced
Into a stony wilderness of the heart,
Under a hostile and a red-clawed sun;
All that dry day, until the darkness fell,
I heard him going, and shouting among the canyons.
But I, struck backward from the eastern gate,
Had turned aside, obscure,
Beneath the unfriendly silence of the moon,
My long white fingers on a small carved lute.
There was a forest, and faces known in childhood
Rose unexpected from the mirrored pools;

The trees had hands to clutch my velvet shoulders,
And birds of fever sang among the branches;
Till the dark vine-boughs, breaking as I seized them,
And dripping blood, cried out with my own voice:
'I also have known thirst, and the wanderer's terror!...'

But I had lost my friend and the mountain paths;
And if there might have been another meeting –
The new sun rising in a different sky,
Having repaired his light in the streams of Ocean,
And the moon, white and maternal, going down
Over the virgin hills – it is too late
Ever to find it now.

And though it was in May that the reptile guns
And breeze-fly bullets took my friend away,
It is no time to forge a delicate idyll
Of the young shepherd, stricken, prone among
The flowers of Spring, heavy with morning dew,
And emblematic blood of dying gods;
Or that head pillowed on a wave's white fleece,
Softly drowning in a Celtic sea.
This was more harsh and meaningless than winter.

But now, at last, I dare avow my terror
Of the pale vampire by the cooling grate;
The enemy face that doubled every loved one;
My secret fear of him and his cold heroes;
The meaning of the dream
Which was so fraught with trouble for us both;
And how, through this long autumn
(Sick and tempestuous with another sorrow)
His spirit, vexed, fluttered among my thoughts,
A bird returning to the darkened window –

The hard-eyed albatross with scissor bill.
And I would ask his pardon for this weakness.

But he is gone where no hallooing voice
Nor beckoning hand may ever call him back;
And what is ours of him
Must speak impartially for all the world;
There is no personal word remains for me,
And I pretend to find no meaning here.
Though I might guess that other Singer's wisdom
Who saw in Death a dark immaculate flower,
And tenderness in every falling autumn,
This abstract music will not bring again
My friend to his warm room:
Inscrutable the darkness covers him.

To the Mermaid at Zennor

Half fish, half fallen angel, none of you
Human at all – cease your lust's
Cold and insatiate crying from the tangled bay;
Nor, sea-hag, here
Stretch webbed and skinny fingers for your prey.

This is a hideous and a wicked country,
Sloping to hateful sunsets and the end of time,
Hollow with mine-shafts, naked with granite, fanatic
With sorrow. Abortions of the past
Hop through these bogs; black-faced, the villagers
Remember burnings by the hewn stones.

Only the saints,
Drifting on oak-leaves over the Irish Sea,
To sing like pipits from their crannied cells
With a thin stream of praise; who hear the Jennifer
Sob for her sins in a purgatory of foam –
Only these holy men
Can send you slithering from the chancel steps,
And wriggling back to your sunken paradise
Among the hollow-eyed and the capsized.

JAMES KIRKUP [1918–2009]

Love and Apocalypse: for Leo

The ugly cataracts
bomb the revolving ravens of the precipice.

In the bolt-upright sepulchres
the organ's crimson motors now emerge
like wedding-monsters
electrocuting no one.

You for a while
cover a whole book with your hair.

But even you, prophetic miracle,
over the remnants of the world's collapse
hold only rival sway,
knowing the awful end must loosen all
and he come with nothing, voiceless, lover of none.

A Correct Compassion

To Mr Philip Allison, after watching him perform a Mitral Stenosis Valvulotomy in the General Infirmary at Leeds.

Cleanly, sir, you went to the core of the matter.
Using the purest kind of wit, a balance of belief and art,
You with a curious nervous elegance laid bare
The root of life, and put your finger on its beating heart.

The glistening theatre swarms with eyes, and hands, and eyes.
On green-clothed tables, ranks of instruments transmit a sterile gleam.
The masks are on, and no unnecessary smile betrays
A certain tension, true concomitant of calm.

Here we communicate by looks, though words,
Too, are used, as in continuous historic present
You describe our observations and your deeds.
All gesture is reduced to its result, an instrument.

She who does not know she is a patient lies
Within a tent of green, and sleeps without a sound
Beneath the lamps, and the reflectors that devise
Illuminations probing the profoundest wound.

A calligraphic master, improvising, you invent
The first incision, and no poet's hesitation
Before his snow-blank page mars your intent:
The flowing stroke is drawn like an uncalculated inspiration.

A garland of flowers unfurls across the painted flesh.
With quick precision the arterial forceps click.
Yellow threads are knotted with a simple flourish.
Transfused, the blood preserves its rose, though it is sick.

Meters record the blood, measure heart-beats, control the breath.
Hieratic gesture: scalpel bares a creamy rib; with pincer knives
The bone quietly is clipped, and lifted out. Beneath,
The pink, black-mottled lung like a revolted creature heaves,

Collapses; as if by extra fingers is neatly held aside
By two ordinary egg-beaters, kitchen tools that curve
Like extraordinary hands. Heart, laid bare, silently beats. It can hide
No longer, yet is not revealed. – 'A local anaesthetic in the cardiac nerve'.

Now, in firm hands that quiver with a careful strength,
The knife feels through the heart's transparent skin; at first,
Inside the pericardium, slit down half its length,
The heart, black-veined, swells like a fruit about to burst,

But goes on beating, love's poignant image bleeding at the dart
Of a more grievous passion, as a bird, dreaming of flight, sleeps on
Within its leafy cage. – 'It generally upsets the heart
A bit, though not unduly, when I make the first injection'.

Still, still the patient sleeps, and still the speaking heart is dumb.
The watchers breathe an air far sweeter, rarer than the room's.
The cold walls listen. Each in his own blood hears the drum
She hears, tented in green, unfathomable calms.

'I make a purse-string suture here, with a reserve
Suture, which I must make first, and deeper,
As a safeguard, should the other burst. In the cardiac nerve
I inject again a local anaesthetic. Could we have fresh towels to cover

All these adventitious ones. Now can you all see.
When I put my finger inside the valve, there may be a lot
Of blood, and it may come with quite a bang. But I let it flow,
In case there are any clots, to give the heart a good clean-out.

Now can you give me every bit of light you've got'.
We stand on the benches, peering over his shoulder.
The lamp's intensest rays are concentrated on an inmost heart.
Someone coughs. – 'If you have to cough, you will do it outside this theatre.' – 'Yes, sir.'

'How's she breathing, Doug? Do you feel quite happy?' – 'Yes, fairly
Happy'. – 'Now. I am putting my finger in the opening of the valve.
I can only get the tip of my finger in. – It's gradually
Giving way. – I'm inside. – No clots. – I can feel the valve

Breathing freely now around my finger, and the heart working.
Not too much blood. It opened very nicely.
I should say that anatomically speaking
This is a perfect case. – Anatomically.

For, of course, anatomy is not physiology'.
We find we breathe again, and hear the surgeon hum.
Outside, in the street, a car starts up. The heart regularly
Thunders. – 'I do not stitch up the pericardium.

It is not necessary'. – For this is imagination's other place,
Where only necessary things are done, with the supreme and grave
Dexterity that ignores technique; with proper grace
Informing a correct compassion, that performs its love, and makes it live.

DEREK STANFORD [1918–2008]

Peter

He stood by an open fire to warm his hands
as I have seen them stand in Nissen huts
by the fitful orange flicker of a stove,
talking to NCOs – a regular buddy –
whilst, outside, April in its calloused hand
showed to the world a sprig of frozen almond.

His sword had been put up; its baptism
in faith and violence, in the scuffle, forgotten.
The cock had not yet crowed. His nerve was gone:
he sought to merge himself with other men.

Vain travesty! Upon the fallible sand
of shifting instinct Time had planned a rock –
absolute bulwark, enemy to time,
history's shield resisting history's shock.

But before blood could find the strength of stone,
Peter needs first must suffocate, head down.

MAURICE LINDSAY [1918–2005]

Earl Magnus Before Haakon on Egilsay

> *Now it must be told of Earl Haakon that he summoned to him a large force and had eight warships, all well manned for instant action. And when the army was mustered, the Earl makes it known to them that he means so to settle up with Earl Magnus at their meeting that they would not both of them be rulers over the Orkneys thereafter... Earl Magnus with his band of men arrived first in Egilsay. And when they espied Earl Haakon coming they saw that he had eight warships: then Magnus knew for certain that there was foul play afoot.*
>
> Orkneyinga Saga, Chapter XLVIII
> April 15th, 1117
> (Translated by Dr A.B. Taylor).

I am your liege, your victim and your lamb,
my brother Haakon; not because this day
your careless army walls my followers,
fingering bright accoutrements of death;
nor even though my quiet life looms forfeit
to stake a crack within your pride's high steeple
and prop your rule upon the unwilling people.

Your liege, for blood from my once chasmed skull
would swim an endless valley round your soul
and drown the clotted entrails of your throat.
Your victim, since the channels of my eyes
are yours for stopping with a clumsy shard,
my body's boundaries are yours for breaking,
the gestures of my limbs yours for the taking.

I am your lamb upon the fallen tree,
the stretched skin of your sudden revelation;
I am the sum of your forgotten sun,
the rooted power of your revolution;
the silly lamb whose eyes are oceans' void,
with sacrificial symbols on his side;
I am your white Christ now re-crucified.

When a man stands edged by the affrighted cliff
of his own indecision, and the cup-like hearts of brothers
await the ripples from each loaded word,
his syllables fall certain seeds of sorrow,
or force withdrawal of that private fence
which separates his griefs from others' envy
and shields his weeping from their ample loves.

When a man stands fronting the ghosts of his own violence,
the act is hidden in its bleak beyond
and shaded with a mocking shape of virtue.
Each minute, Haakon, houses all man's lusts,
and only the heart which pulls an arrowed purpose
can pierce the substances of stray desires
to reach that solid truth where it aspires.

Greed rocks your will, as deeply passioned seas
baffle white, frothy fury on thin sands,
propound green anger to reluctant shores.
Yet, brother, I would leave these happy islands
rather than blood of mine corrode your bones,
since now you taste the sodden seeds of power
within the drinking of each heady hour.

The winds which sing my murdered breath asunder
over squat islands, the desperate, lonely seas,
and the unsettled continents, are the same winds
that string the warrior's hopes around his dreams.
The helpless wind which shelters rape in Norway,
treachery shuttered in a Scottish glen,
speaks swords of comfort to defeated men.

For me, this life is love, vaster than eye
can fathom, wider than any ear can plan.
My body is a vessel full of sorrow,
your sorrows, and the griefs of every man.
And I have studied how a man should die,
his praying heart hung in its proud, high place,
the map of courage printed on his face.

Therefore against your own best-bettered judgment
hurt me, disrupt this body's ordered pose.
I will accept, since only pure acceptance
succours the dragging nails upon the cross.
I will accept what pains are your betrayal
to free the tight-wrung fabric of your soul
before it tears on God's sharp testing shoal.

If all my words have shrivelled in your rage,
strike, and at least ensure time's infamy.

MURIEL SPARK [1918–2006]

No Need for Shouting (for D.S.)

No need for shouting across the interval
Of mountain and mountain since we are
Nearer than the sun and moon are far.
Here, only distance preserves an ephemeral
Idyllic metaphor.

Whatever imitation between lover and lover passes
Implicitly as bird or stream defined,
This falters about my fain, my leisureless
And word-bedevilled mind
As the wind concerns the eddying grasses.

No need, in any case, for shouting. Praise
Moves like an elegy between steeple and steeple tolling,
Stilling the natural voice.
So I am dumbfounded by our mutual days,
Amazed beneath the sun and in the night's consoling.

TOM SCOTT [1919–1995]

The Bride

I dreamed a luesome dream o ye yestreen.
Ye stuid in dawan fields agin a purpour lift
And a tree o floueran starns raise frae your croun.
Lown as a simmer sea ye stuid, your breists
Keekan throu the lintlocks o your hair,
And ye were leaman wi a radiance eterne,
Ye, my ever-virgin, ever-breedan bride.

Your waddin-kiss, the warld your body is,
Are brenned ayebydan in my benmaist hert
As Psyche's oil in Eros' shouther brenned.

Wap your love-spells round me evermair,
Bind me ti you wi your daethless love,
My queyn, my queen, dochter o oor God.
Lead me on throu evergrouwan licht, and be
My love, my ain, the guide o the guid in me.

In burns o immortal rain baptise me, love.

PETER WELLS [1919–2013]

Lament for Victory

Since there are no more beaches to conquer, and slow
Poverty has struck down those whom no leaves cover:
Since the quiet shell, the impenetrable factory have uttered
Their final proclamation, and no gun
Echoes again the weeping, the defeated:
Since under the snow the silent bodies menace,
Like iron manacles, grinding all hope, the inconsolable losses;
Since all is fallen, now not even the flowers shall perish,
But the tired women shall come out on to the snow with crosses.

ERNEST FROST [1919–1986]

Elegiac Portrait, Italy, 1944

I

Holding the funeral air, in a black gown bell-blown
from the dead musicians, from the ungainly vine, from parched
unprofitable ground, from dark and double-spinning
dark, from dawn to death – holding the funeral air
The easy sun stampedes across the wound. The sea
splinters on sticks of sight. Thrown up are glass
retrieving hands, thrown up are glandular long swells

of the contrapuntal light. And all inside the grief
of the funeral air, the black and shedding air,
are leaves cracked and devoured by easy sliding suns,
and the guns of daybreak. Slowly, small fires
seep through our sleep. Cock-crow at black, at four o'clock,
grins in the soldier's sweat. Fear tumbles down a cloud.

The sleeper turns.

II

And purple flowers are netted on the brain,
and the sick arm hanging from a wall, holding
purple the sprawling names of the purple
flowers. Talk in deep water, in cylindrical Time's
black base, and at the well's dead centre, talk
of the purple catharsis of flowers, the minute
veins under a microscope, the stamen like a tower,
and into purple all divisions flow.

Being and behaving,
being and just and beautiful and sane, believing
that purple breaks from pain… O believing that
nothing could ever be the same, pausing under
the innumerable cities and statues grown over
and dead beneath these flowers.

Because of the name,
because of the name of war, and the name of power
a city exploded and never rose again.

III

O bread and music be given to the famished mind,
and splendid in history the double-rising rose announce
how, in the violent other-rose of the inhuman bombardment,
the modern Dante in rags of gold words shall arise
and the innumerable mimosa of the operatic nightfall
descend, descend upon human decency and human tenderness.
O bread and music on history be larger than the tyrants
here, and within us. And in all Europe's sadness.
O bread and music deliver us from evil, and uncover
holy the landscape of our love for one another.

O bread and music save us from hunger and death
in this beautiful peninsula of the heart lying in water.

MAURICE JAMES CRAIG [1919–2011]

Ballad to a Traditional Refrain

I

Red brick in the suburbs, white horse on the wall,
Eyetalian marbles in the City Hall:
O stranger from England, why stand so aghast?
May the Lord in His mercy be kind to Belfast.

II

This jewel that houses our hopes and our fears
Was knocked up from the swamp in the last hundred years;

But the last shall be first and the first shall be last;
May the Lord in His mercy be kind to Belfast.

III

We swore by King William there'd never be seen
An all-Irish Parliament at College Green
So at Stormont we're nailin' our flag to the mast.
May the Lord in His mercy be kind to Belfast.

IV

O the bricks they will bleed, and the rain it will weep,
And the damp Lagan fog lull the city to sleep;
It's to hell with the future and live on the past;
May the Lord in His mercy be kind to Belfast.

PRUNELLA CLOUGH [1919–1999]

To the 200-Inch Telescope

Theirs was a molten uncertainty – the slow
cooling, moulding the plan of a geometer –
a hope, bound by its glassy diameter
that by degree harder there should be no flaw.
For they too, grinding the grey specular
lens, saw the dust of precision blown
like stars over the polished arc, soon
aluminium-sprayed, oracle of a secular
temple, mounted in the clear air
and open dome at Palomar. Deeper still
in light-years the explosive suns will

print their evidence, plotting here
the curve, the intersection we have wintered
of time unbounded and time splintered.

East Coast

So rusts the summer sorrel
          iron at the hinge of the door
where the surf breaks over the boom in the channel
                    and the boats lie dry ashore
                    away from the wave peril.

The high gull's wing-wheel falls
          shadowing, the sunglare flaking
the names painted on the woodgrain of the hulls –
                    fishermen's sons – making
                    a vermilion dynasty dull.

And there the metal stantions
          harrow the shore; the tide
smooths the tank-indented sand, but no erosion
                    can efface the concrete where so wide
                    encircling runs the bastion.

Those in the guns' orbit have
          monuments; for those who fell
before, the old wire breaks, but new perspectives
                    coil a wiry helix like a shell
                    where sounds of battle interweave.

For they who wait, no more
          galaxies of scales lie spotted
in the nets hung from the wall, yet still their
                    fingers weave, daylight knotted
                    in the dark of age and war.

EUGENE WATTERS [1919–1982]

from *The Week-End of Dermot and Grace*

Look Dermot, how the sun flames on the beach
That was as silk to our bare feet yesterday.
Every pool is a saucer of Greek fire.
With which they came birdbeaked and crucified
Achieving their civilisation
In terms of a sanitary accommodation
Upon remembered streets of Crete, Tyre,
Brick, cane and corrugation. *Kyrie*
Eleison. Who fell in the Easter rising
Before the last fallout with some few sins
Gone in the flame of the flower. Music of violins
Curling and cupping within lucent sheets
Stamen and pistil and the quick dust that clings
To the ideal ghost as about a nucleus.
That as a diver going clean
Into the screaming shocked sea
Brings the long morning under
This humped slumped salt virginity
Half dawn, half death, birdhaunted history.

EMYR HUMPHREYS [BORN 1919; LIVES IN WALES]

Cowardice

In journeyings my weak soul makes
And breaks the pestilence of swarming sin
I am the courier through the burning lakes
That bears the body with the message in.

I am the field of war, where good and bad
Mingle and batter and break, striving for place
Like well-matched warriors making an Iliad
Behind the fixed flesh barrier of my face.

Though battles and adventures over again
Possess this celluloid within my skull
Bones must escape the circumstantial rain
Blood must remain unspilt; flesh plentiful.

The play should stay in print, avoiding Action
Or else the text will suffer in translation.

Humble Song

Tonight, before I went to bed
Alone but reasonably fed
By an unfriendly hand,
A terrible humility
Rose like a temperature in me.

Then every word and every act
Seemed superfluous, inexact
And every thought like a lost sheep
Shivered before the impenetrably deep
Shadow of nihilist night

A numen lurking in the blood
Felt, feared, but barely understood
Suggested only this
Thesis, antithesis:

I am a sacrifice for all
That little children may grow tall
I am the murderer who waits
To shoot the prophet at the gates
A grain of cosmic sand
In an almighty hand:

Or in an unknown office drawer
My life lies waiting for
A clerk's impersonal thumb
My synthesis seemed true
From any point of view –

A doctor with his scalpel
Eyeing my tender navel
A nurse beside my bed
Grinning at what he said
And I lie passive, helpless, stiff
Caught in an anaesthetic 'If' –

Tonight the wind blows from the East
Cutting the soldier's broken breast
Let each tear help to swell the flood
Washing away the map of blood
While I like any frightened boy
Clutch at my childhood's ragged toy
Running with heavy rooted feet
Down night's apocalyptic street.

ROLAND GANT [1919–1993]

The Wedding

Because there was no moon
our young sister was married
by the light of the stars.
She walked slowly the length
of the aisle of the river,
the stones arched above her
and the windows were water
patterned with lilies
and garlands of reeds.
She walked with her bridegroom
down the nave of the sea
to the peal of the waves
and lightly-flung sand grains.
We called to her, called to her
and the echo returned to us
from the vaults of the ocean.
Because there was no moon
our young sister was married

by the light of the stars
and her heart was closed
within a light ring of coral.

JOHN BAYLISS [1919–2008]

Apocalypse and Resurrection

I have seen the white horsemen riding to hell
with their legions fast as light, fierce and inevitable
as volcanic lava, molten frost, invincible
as the great stone that falls from the hill:

and the Cenotaph is breaking in Whitehall
under the artillery of the dead,
and in a thousand parks the grimed memorials
sway in the wind of the counted battalions they record,
and the names march into the Council Chamber
into the home, the betrayer's bed,
and the mayor is strangled with his scarlet cord.

And the politician with his great house of promises
runs screaming out of the falling cards,
and the bishop is choked with his warring words:
and the skeleton walks into the brothel
demanding his due and paying the price with a gold
ring that is green from lying long in the earth:

and the great towers topple and crack
as the flat shadows of birds fight
over the crushed flesh, and the white

flash of the moon between clouds
betrays the cold eye watching, the old
inimical star that has driven men mad.

But before they come there is a dry rustle of leaves
and the wind turns a little from the hill,
and hands come out of the tombs in Chiswick churchyard
and slip into the hands of passers-by,
and all the drugs of cassia and nard
are insufficient to stop the Egyptian mummy
walking out of the British Museum into the Strand.

And in Chiswick House the madmen are throwing their clocks
into the lake, and the wild clack of the geese
echoes the wheels of black coaches drawn up on the gravel:
and dark flowers are breaking the concrete roads of Kew,
and the bridge is burning above the ebony river
in an arc of fire: and the terrace to Richmond Park
is covered with silk and lace and satin and red
and blue and green and silver dresses, that preen
and flutter and pause as they did the day they died,
and the dress was laid in the press and the wearer laid
in the marble vault smoothing her last brocade.

On these, on us, on the dust of centuries,
the image of glass, or gilt, or porcelain,
the moving figures of Madame Tussaud's that walk
only at night, now walking their last domain,
on these the white wind rustled, the raving horse
reared to the sky and fell like a fountain of ice
covering all: the stone and the dark remain
sole effigies of all the creatures that ran
or fought or dreamed throughout the dissident years,
and the white horsemen who passed have ended their wars.

HAMISH HENDERSON [1919–2002]

from *Opening of an Offensive*

Armour has foregathered, snuffling
through tourbillions of fine dust.
The crews don't speak much. They've had
last brew-up before battle. The tawny
deadland lies in a silence
not yet smashed by salvoes.
No sound reaches us
from the African constellations.

[...]

They move forward into no man's land, a vibrant sounding board.

          As they advance
the guns push further murderous music.
Is this all they will hear, this raucous apocalypse?
The spheres knocking in the night of Heaven?
The drummeling of overwhelming niagara?
No! For I can hear it! Or is it?... tell
Me that I can hear it! Now – listen!

          Yes, hill and shieling
sea-loch and island, hear it, the yell
of your war-pipes, scaling sound's mountains
guns' thunder drowning in their soaring swell!

from *Tenth Elegy*

So I turn aside in the benighted deadland
to perform a duty, noting an outlying
grave, or restoring a fallen cross-piece.
Remembrancer.
            And shall sing them who amnestied
escaped from the tumult to stumble across sand-dunes
and darken their waves in the sea, the deliverer.

Run, stumble and fall in their instant of agony
past burnt-out brennpunkt, along hangdog dannert.
Here gutted, or stuck through the throat like Buonconte,
or charred to grey ash, they are caught in one corral.
We fly from their scorn, but they close all the passes:
their sleep's our unrest, we lie bound in their inferno –
this alliance must be vaunted and affirmed, lest they condemn us!
Lean seedlings of lament spring like swordsmen around us;
the coronach scales white arêtes. Bitter keening
of women goes up by the solitary column.
Denounce and condemn! Either build for the living
love, patience and powder to absolve these tormented,
or else choke in the folds of their black-edged vendetta!
Run, stumble and fall in our desert of failure,
impaled, unappeased. And inhabit that desert
of canyon and dream – till we carry to the living
blood, fire and red flambeaux of death's proletariat.
Take iron in your arms! At last, spanning this history's
apollyon chasm, proclaim them the reconciled.

PATRICIA BEER [1919–1997]

Movable Feast

Moon and the calendar swung the feast
Gold as a roundabout through the spring.
Children we saw the season fling
The dice of days to the watching priest.

He asked for our slender human tears
Till the moon shone cold as a daffodil
On the dancing earth where Easter fell
And we rolled our grief down the sloping years.

How could we know and we so tame
That the helter-skelter of time stood high
In the fairground, down from the smoking sky
To the roots of Pentecost under the flame,

And how could we bear at point of noon
The sun-high truth where the shadow ceased
Or bid to our movable human feast
All the calendar, all the moon?

ALEX COMFORT [1920–2000]

Hoc Est Corpus

I who am nothing, and this tissue
steer, find in my servant still my maker,
rule and obey, as flame to candle mated:
whom bone has conjured, Banquo shall the Bard
command, the marble rule Pygmalion.
Did this tower build me then who am its garrison?

Strange that in me the shadow
moving the substance speaks: strange that such air
pulls the blue sinew, whom the blood maintains
whom the heart's coming slight defection
shall spill, speaks now and holds
time like a permanent stone, its cold weight judging.

from *The Sleeping Princess: A Journey with Figures*

Flowers and fields, gates, tenements,
the ruffled shops, the graveyard, the pool
for children's boats, the park with serpentine paths,
gardens sitting like swallows along a wire:
the cooling towers grouped by the creased river
under a flat light brightening as day grows.
Quitting these, then, we are carried between
diffident cattle into the cup of country.
Sheep run from our shadow, insolent birds stare.

[…]

Placid country, country of marriages,
real under our strange journey, making
the churches under chestnuts scatter their guests

country of couples, making the platform
run with leavetaking faces, wishes
that the window turns to lips, and these fall back.

[…]

Those who travel with me
from insignificant stations
that stick in the country's throat –
cases on luggage racks,
this bucket dipped in the nation
two who play cards: one with a child: one with an axe –

carry their trades and chances
by cord or under arm
white eyes that watch a speaker
silent with one another,
privately, willing to learn
nothing, receive no news, admit no brother.

Do I carry my trade, or they
smell and distrust my verse?
If the hard crust broke, would they ask
'What have you to say?
Things are come to a pass –
the train runs on, whether we play or refuse to play.

What do you want? We sit
and wait for it. So do you'.
I look across at the hands –

four that shuffle the pack,
two are the child's, and two
holding the child, and two for the axe propped on the rack:

and think: look down at your own –
feel the tongue in your mouth.
My trade is shrunken down
to a negative, giving the lie
to the lie that means your death.
You in your private silence have left me the cry:

Mother is making your bed
in the Agamemnonian dark.
Your four hands shuffle your fate.
The evil axe is your own.
The papers that screen you bark
for your death, and you leave me to bellow alone

the schedule of First Aid
the procedure in case of fire.
'What can we do? Where go?
The time is out of joint –
there is nothing possible here –
our hands are single, our voice and your voice faint –

we may be healed in the end –
perhaps they are telling the truth –
we must Stand Up for our Rights –
we never have had a chance –
there is no tongue in our mouth –
the fine is forty shillings for the first offence!'

This is the work I do –
I gather your scattered No

your inarticulate salvage
of bloody-mindedness
drive your doubts in a row
as a fence between you and the eyeless, voiceless, press

of those who were Citizens
who waited another week,
whose poor disguises failed,
who did not speak soon enough,
who thought it useless to speak,
whose No was killed by custom, and they by custom killed.

Give me this for my work.
I ask you to speak, not hear.
I am your audience. Give
the disobedient word
that will open history's ear
like the prince's kiss that woke, and the sleepers stirred.

GERVASE STEWART [1920–1941]

He Whom I Have Not Seen

He whom I have not seen is my destroyer,
He wrecks my days who might have been my father,
Or, with his flame makes fire of my endeavour,
Who might have been my lover.

Man whom I do not know maps out my morrow,
Weighs up my strength who has not felt my marrow,
Or scrawls war's signature across my meadow,
Who does not fear my sorrow.

He whom I might have helped hinders my future,
Splinters my stage who will not let me feature,
Or pictures me merely as numbered creature,
Who calls me failure.

JOHN GALLEN [C 1920–1947]

A Little Lyricism on a New Occasion

Not hard as hard is, but hard as soft is,
but red-berry pulp lapped in no-spored glistering –
dreams, my child – those were lips in a dream.

Not mind as mind is, but mind as self is
but warm shoulders in the arm-vice, warm thought in the eye-vice:
dreams I should say – O yes! love in a dream.

Not world as world is, but world as wish is
but the long-suffering of 'I' at last lost, lip-puffed-by:
dreams no doubt – there is no need of courage

nor of anything but dreaming, in a dream.

DAVID WRIGHT [1920–1994]

By Jordan and the Water

I John by Jordan and the water
upon the angle of my hand
the dove of heaven made an altar
my finger in an angry land
and swung my vision to the quarter
reared Zion out of Babylon.

I shaped his message on the water
I scored his sentence on the sand
I John engraved in stone and thunder
the angle of the sun and moon
with cipher of the thirst and hunger
reared Zion out of Babylon.

The star of morning was my daughter
the horn of Patmos Babylon
shattered and shattered fane and altar
within the girdle of the doom
I saw where Jordan and the water
reared Zion out of Babylon.

Five South African Poems: I

Each time I return to Johannesburg it is summer,
And clouds hang with black the stage of the sky,
So I perceive the auditors prepared for tragedy,
Ready for lightning, where a harp of thunder

Leans towards Magaliesberg. Does my childhood
Lie before those mountains, where Pretoria
Veils her white facades with jacaranda
Below their shoulders? From Orange Grove

I'd look all morning at the distance laid between,
The bare areas, undeveloped altitudes,
And plant their furlongs with imagined woods
To be grown in the fields between Magaliesberg and my home.

Over them stoop and bend the throats of summer
Each time I return to Johannesburg. Over them
I see and hear a portentous requiem
Performed, for each return, by my native weather,

For burial of the closing distances.
The scale grows less. I see the mountains near
My home at each return, dwindle and wither
The imagined woods as death to birth advances.

Canons Ashby

County of squares and spires, in the middle of England,
Where with companions I was used to rove,
Country containing the cedar of John Dryden,
Cedar, in whose shadow of thunder and love
I saw those Caroline lawns, and musical
I heard, inaudible, those waters fall, fall

Triumphs and miseries, last poet of a golden
Order, and under whose laurel I'd desire
To plant a leaf of bay, and by whose building
To tune irregular strings, the stronger lyre

Plunging, a swan to alight, into a clear
Music of language I delight to hear.

Not a hundred yards from where my substance wastes
Nightly in London, John Dryden died on tick.
The air clouded, and in his garden gusts
Shook that cedar tree; as I watched its branches flick
In a windy prolegomenon to autumn
While a sky marshalled engines to a storm,

I no longer heard those falling waters fall,
Silence like Iris descended from a cloud,
And lawns grew dark, as that once musical
Shadow of a cedar faded in the loud
Shades of thunder-cumuli on the grass,
Till we left the garden empty as it was.

On the Death of an Emperor Penguin in Regent's Park

A proletarian, unlikely bird, no monarch,
Whose northern relation, the Gare-fowl or Great Auk,
One hundred years has been extinct on this island;
An ugly, blubber-jacketed, wingless giant
Laboriously transported from his desert of ice,
His house of hurricanes (uncomfortable birthplace!
Cold and insanitary, where ocean hardens!)
Has perished in the Zoological Gardens.
Tell, masochistic martyr, what ailed you?
Here there is care and comfort; what can have killed you?
Speak, shade! Were your keepers neglecting your welfare?
Did you lack anything purchasable with silver?
O stupid, ungrateful bird! Blubber and feather!
To die of desire for freedom and bad weather!

For the perch where you, pegged to a glacier's bitter stone
Outlast an Antarctic unending cyclone,
And watch, neither superb nor able, from below
A smashed world whirl away in stinging snow.

ROBERT GREACEN [1920–2008]

The Glorious Twelfth (12 July, 1943)

You will remember that the Twelfth was always dry,
That rain followed the day after, some said as Judgment,
While others argued that drums of Ulster stirring
Pulled out the corded wetness from our local skies.
Four years ago we heard them last, heard the thunder
Smouldering through the ribboned streets towards the battle
In the fields of Finaghy. There was fire then,
Fire in our throats, fire beaten out from our cities,
Cold, distant, strongly arid in the normal weather:
Four years ago since last we heard the drums' thunder,
Since the Orange banners looped in gay procession
And bands of flute and fife, of brass and silver
Played hell to the Pope and immortality to William –
To William, Prince of Orange, defender and avenger,
To William, the stiff Dutch Protestant who saved us
From villainous James, the tyrant Stuart King.

Remember 1690, remember the ancient wrongs of Rome,
Remember Derry, Aughrim, Enniskillen and the Boyne,
The glorious Boyne in Ireland, where the Pope was overcome,
Remember the Maiden City and the breaking of her boom.

These were my people marching on the streets,
Released from inhibition and resolved to keep the faith.
Four years have passed since Ulster opened up her heart,
And toasted her deliverance from the Seven Hills,
Four years since fire has run swift rivers into Europe
From Dunkirk to Briansk, from Naples to Novgorod,
From Caucasus to Clyde, from Warsaw to Belfast.
And now, in Derry and Downpatrick, no Ulstermen are marching
To the rustle of their banners and the flogging of their drums.
Our red-brick cities have their blackened skeletons,
Our people carry the public and the personal wound.

Forgotten 1690, forgotten the ancient wrongs of Rome,
Forgotten Derry, Aughrim, Enniskillen and the Boyne,
The glorious Boyne in Ireland where the Pope was overcome,
Forgotten the Maiden City and the breaking of her boom.

You will remember that the Twelfth was always dry,
While now in Italy the bloods of Continents are joined,
While now the Russian plains are stacked with corpses,
Rotting in the Red sun, feeding plagues to common rats…
But after carnage there will be music; after death will be hope,
After the horror of the day will come the evening dream,
After hatred's harvest joy will march, shrouded, to Finaghy.

LESLIE PHILLIPS [BORN C 1920]

Submarine Victims

For that cold dawn
I had bartered a cradled mist,
Floated down the seething dark
To the pale sea face,
Where nurtured in my silent trespass
The fashioned arc of the sky had faced
Its augured sun.

That eager sun
Had folded back the sifting waves,
Planted fast the resonant tower
Of curtained doubt,
In which my darkening heart still beat
Over the unconsidered lives
Of drowning men.

Those dreaming men
Had bubbled up their wasting breath
Purged their bones of encumbering life
On the green sea bed,
Where rounded on the stolen mud
Their fingers clutched the death
Of that cold dawn.

BARBARA NORMAN [1920–1972]

Lament

One woman sorrowing
in one lone covenant:
for ever the heart
of her bright Archer rent.

All arrows spent:
empty the quiver,
and hanging-down the hand,
the bow of the light body
broken in a barren land;
                                        she went,
thinking of an earth whereon
fierce feathers fall
and none lament.

KEITH DOUGLAS [1920–1944]

Canoe

Well, I am thinking this may be my last
summer, but cannot lose even a part
of pleasure in the old-fashioned art of
idleness. I cannot stand aghast

at whatever doom hovers in the background;
while grass and buildings and the somnolent river,
who know they are allowed to last for ever,
exchange between them the whole subdued sound

of this hot time. What sudden fearful fate
can deter my shade wandering next year
from a return? Whistle and I will hear
and come again another evening, when this boat

travels with you alone toward Iffley:
as you lie looking up for thunder again,
this cool touch does not betoken rain;
it is my spirit that kisses your mouth lightly.

How to Kill

Under the parabola of a ball,
a child turning into a man,
I looked into the air too long.
The ball fell in my hand, it sang
in the closed fist: *Open Open*
Behold a gift designed to kill.

Now in my dial of glass appears
the soldier who is going to die.
He smiles, and moves about in ways
his mother knows, habits of his.
The wires touch his face: I cry
NOW. Death, like a familiar, hears

and look, has made a man of dust
of a man of flesh. This sorcery
I do. Being damned, I am amused
to see the centre of love diffused
and the waves of love travel into vacancy.
How easy it is to make a ghost.

The weightless mosquito touches
her tiny shadow on the stone,
and with how like, how infinite
a lightness, man and shadow meet.
They fuse. A shadow is a man
when the mosquito death approaches.

On a Return from Egypt

To stand here in the wings of Europe
disheartened, I have come away
from the sick land where in the sun lay
the gentle sloe-eyed murderers
of themselves, exquisites under a curse;
here to exercise my depleted fury.

For the heart is a coal, growing colder
when jewelled cerulean seas change
into grey rocks, grey water-fringe,
sea and sky altering like a cloth
till colour and sheen are gone both:
cold is an opiate of the soldier.

And all my endeavours are unlucky explorers
come back, abandoning the expedition;
the specimens, the lilies of ambition
still spring in their climate, still unpicked:
but time, time is all I lacked
to find them, as the great collectors before me.

The next month, then, is a window
and with a crash I'll split the glass.
Behind it stands one I must kiss,

person of love or death
a person or a wraith,
I fear what I shall find.

EDWIN MORGAN [1920–2010]

The Sleights of Darkness

One nightmare after cinderfall
Idiocy in a slumber took me aside
To see my friend in his golden fell
Stumble at the handle of fiends'-hovel
By the feral riverside.

Blown like a quill to that fell lintel
He fumbled with bolts to mingle loneliness
With the waiting loneliness till little by little
Meeting by his fever the lascivious toll
He should feel fiend-homeliness.

And yet if all flesh was standing
As thick as smoke from wall to wall
And if love like gold was seen ascending
Through the valley of the blood and the understanding
What would suffice of it all

To my friend in his fleshly desolation?
Misery strides along my daydream
Whenever I re-unlatch his destruction.
His face at the fiends' sill is confusion,
Pale as the breaking stream.

Bitter vision, not of wishes!
Let me not find his heart at bay
Or laid with innocence in ashes,
Or if I must, let our lost riches
Of trust be all we must pay!

Slates flash out on the tawny gable;
Windows strain to the sinking sun;
The mavis drowses on its fable
Of the glory of day till the last feeble
Knot of its song is undone.

I strain and flash and fable too,
From the valid twilight before surrender.
Against the Night that scars the true
And mocks the lonely two by two,
Now love be my defender!

from *Stanzas of the Jeopardy*

It may be at midday, limousines in cities, the groaning
Derrick and hissing hawser alive at dockyards,
Liners crawling with heat-baked decks, their élite
Drinking languid above the hounded turbines,
Doorways and crossroads thronged with a hundred rendezvous,
Planes low over spire and cupola with screaming
Jet-streams or soaring inaudible in disembodied calm,
Plough-teams on headlands in the sweat of noon, the warm
Earth up-ruffled swarming for crow and gull,
Boys whistling and calling at play in the sea-caves,
Cables humming, telephonists sighing, sirens
Wailing twelve from workshop and factory, tar
Bubbling in the skin of the street, shopfronts shimmering,

In Times Square, Leicester Square, Red Square – that the roar, the labour
The onset and the heat, the engine and the flurry and the errand,
The plane and the phone and the plough and the farm, the farmer
And the stoker and the airman and the docker and the shopper and the boy
Shall all be called to a halt:
In the middle of the day, and in the twinkling of an eye.

[...]

'Shall the trumpet sound before the suns have cooled?
Shall there not be portents of blood, sea-beds laid bare,
Concrete and girder like matchwood in earthquake and whirlwind?
Shall we not see the angels, or the creeping ice-cap, or the moon
Falling, or the wandering star, feel veins boiling
Or fingers freezing or the wind thickening with wings?'
The earth may spin beyond apocalypse;
Long before entropy the worlds may stop.
The heart praises its own intentions, while the moment,
The neighbour, the need, the face of love and the tears
Have passed unseized, as some day they will pass
Beyond all action, beyond despair and redemption,
When matter has uttered its last sound, when the eye
That roved around the universe goes blind, when lips
To lips are numb, when space is rolled away
And time is torn from its rings, and the door of life
Flies open on unimaginable things –
At noon, at midnight, or at no time,
As you receive these verses, O Corinthians.

J.C. HALL [1920–2011]

Journey to London

From the Welsh wick asleep in the globe of winter
I came across England to love and anger,
Came from that mountainous indifference
To where my hopes were, your lips, our danger.

Riding the three ranges, the high midland
Where history piled stone on stone together,
Furnishing from grey stone our politics
And the harsh principles that slay my brother,

Riding the three ranges, I left Malvern
In the flush of sunset and all Oxfordshire
To the veiled glory of its fabled spires,
Came down to darkness and a city's fear.

O London, from the pellucid flame of Wales,
I your citizen and twenty others
Crossed from the Chiltern daylight into darkness,
The night that drowns our enemies and lovers,

Journeyed from grey stone to bombs exploding
Our politics and prayers, to a new anger
Striking from war this poetry. I came
To the heart of love, to the heart of danger.

FRANK THOMPSON [1920–1944]

Day's Journey

Starting at early light from the old fort
Across the dry flaked mud, you remember,
We left the well on our right and the crosses,
Drove west all day through the camel-scrub,
Tossing in convoy like a mobile orchard,
An olive-yard on wheels, irregular,
Spaced over miles: were bombed: were bombed again,
Until the air was dust: drove on due west
Past the sheikh's tomb of stones, past the dry spring,
Until at dusk from the escarpment
Rumbled and boomed the gun's resentment,
Impersonal, the protest of a Titan
Impartially disgusted, while the sun
Signed off in angry flames.
                                        We halted,
Quietly, in close leaguer, half ashamed.

De Amicitia

Odysseus, at the end of life, in your orchards,
Stroking the olive-flowers and the young corn
With thin dry fingers – only in your eyes
The fire that once was the whole man – Odysseus,
Tell me, from all your travels
What do you most remember?

'Not Troy, not any thought of Troy.
Not Polypheme. Not Kalypso. Nor does the sea
Feature except as a well-honoured friend
Smiling a greeting but no invitation.

More than all else I think of the Phaeacians,
Leisure and music in their halls,
The laughter of Alkinous and his tales,
The freedom and the peace of an old friendship,
And Nausikaa,
gay as hibiscus-bloom,
Fresher than dawn, shining unconscious foil
To my other world, to all the dross of manhood'.

IAN FLETCHER [1920–1988]

For My Cousin Lorna, God Keep Her

There's a girl in Germany like a Princess in a tower
With a gold, slow deluge of hair;
We climbed each pear tree in the park.

She knew the highest bough, and could,
Neater than wood-doe, wild heart in the wood,
Race me through paddocks to the crocus bed.

But now the trees are cut, now winter's come,
With Europe one long barrow of the dead;
Letters which inclined meek words are dumb.

There is no whisper arching to tell me where
You bury your slow torrent of gold hair;
Or if, wild-heart, you have run far enough
To escape the hunters without any mark.

JOHN HOLLOWAY [1920–1999]

from *Line and Colour*

Bare new-born people running in the gale.
        Bare and new-born and drowning in the rain
        That strikes their bareness with the force of hail.
'New torments and new people feeling pain'.
        Sometimes a vessel, labouring, through the combing
        Ocean, its soon obliterated lane,
Mounts up across dark wolds of water, foaming
        Greedily up to their fraying summits' gleam:
        These, being deprived of every chance of homing,
Rose through their darkness like men drowned. Now scream,
        Scream bleeding, mandrake, torn up by the spurs,
        Fruitless epiphany of those who stream
Over the passes: for each one transfers
        To his new dark a mere blanched, lifeless day,
        And often as his rightful dream recurs,
Turns back and turns to salt and plods his way
        (Although he knows it is of no avail)
        To that from which it was his curse to stray:
Circe, the mandrake's queen, her people, trail
        Blindly through their new twilight: men transformed.
        What can uprooted creatures do, but fail?

ROY MCFADDEN [1921–1999]

For Retired Rebels

Where is the lean, tight flame of faith,
The vision greater than the four-walled self,
The naked vision bare as death,
Lean, tight and pointed as the moon-trapped wolf?

Must time for ever put grey hairs
On ageing, plump ideals; must the eyes
Come pointless, and the open doors
Clash shutting in the men suckled to mice?

So from the schooled and servile hand
The ledger column sprawls and crucifies
The out-of-time, who will not bend
To burn the incense, bed with compromise.

So in the streets no eyes are turned
Upward to mountains or to passing eyes,
Self-wrapped, aloof, all trebly learned
In cautious counting and safe sacrifice.

O let the clothes drop off, and grass
Flame through the flattened streets, and blossoms fall
Snow-like from the gantries. Pass
From blood and money, and the four-walled hell.

OLIVIA FITZROY [1921–1969]

Fleet Fighter

'Good show!' he said, leaned back his head and laughed.
'They're wizard types!' he said, and held his beer
Steadily, looked at it and gulped it down
Out of its jam-jar, took a cigarette
And blew a neat smoke ring into the air.
'After this morning's prang I've got the twitch;
I thought I'd had it in that teased-out kite'.
His eyes were blue and older than his face,
His single stripe had known a lonely war
But all his talk and movements showed his age.
His whole life was the air and his machine,
He had no thought but of the latest 'mod',
His jargon was of aircraft or of beer.
'And what will you do afterwards?' I said.
Then saw his puzzled face, and caught my breath.
There was no afterwards for him, but death.

LOUIS ADEANE [1921–1979]

For the Lonely

This is our love, these wheels and chains,
Walls, windows, vistas, fettered edge of foam.
Our blood blew red and melted; these remains
Are love cooled down to solid shapes of home.

Yet outside place, beyond our brittle light
Spread fields incredible, the planes of love;
Invisibly they flood towards our sight,
Our little city stands within a wave.

And growing greenly in subversive park
Their secret fountains flourishing impel
The child to feel love falling from the dark,
The wishing girl to dream beside a well.

So leaping flowers in the burning town
May light the marble gardens of our thought
And running visions melt our coldness down
To fire the insurgent freedom of the heart.

GEORGE MACKAY BROWN [1921–1996]

The Death of Peter Esson: Tailor, Town Librarian, Free Kirk Elder

Peter at some immortal cloth, it seemed,
Fashioned and stitched, for so long had he sat
Heraldic on his bench. We never dreamed
It was his shroud that he was busy at.

Well Peter knew, his thousand books would pass
Gray into dust, that still a tinker's tale
As hard as granite and as sweet as grass,
Told over the reeking pipes, outlasts them all.

The Free Kirk cleaves gray houses – Peter's ark
Freighted for heaven, galeblown with psalm and prayer.
The predestined needle quivered on the mark.
The wheel spun true. The seventieth rock was near.

Peter, I mourned. Early on Monday last
There came a wave and stood above your mast.

Elegy

The Magnustide long swords of rain
        Quicken the dust. The ploughman turns
            Furrow by holy furrow
                The liturgy of April.
            What rock of sorrow
        Checks the seed's throb and flow
Now the lark's skein is thrown
                About the burning sacrificial hill?

Cold exiles from that ravished tree
(Fables and animals guard it now)
Whose reconciling leaves
Fold stone, cornstalk and lark,
Our first blood grieves
That never again her lips
Flowering with song we'll see,
Who, winged and bright, speeds down into the dark.

Now let those risers from the dead,
Cornstalks, golden conspirators,
Cry on the careless wind
Ripeness and resurrection;
How the calm wound
Of the girl entering earth's side
Gives back immortal bread
For this year's dust and rain that shall be man.

Chapel Between Cornfield and Shore

Above the ebb, that gray uprooted wall
Was arch and chancel, choir and sanctuary,
A solid round of stone and ritual.
Knox brought all down in his wild hogmanay.

The wave turns round. New ceremonies will thrust
From the thrawn acre where those good stones bleed
Like corn compelling sun and rain and dust
After the crucifixion of the seed.

Restore to that maimed rockpool, when the flood
Sounds all her lucent strings, its ocean dance;
And let the bronze bell nod and cry above

Ploughshare and creel; and sieged with hungry sins
A fisher priest offer our spindrift bread
For the hooked hands and harrowed heart of Love.

T.H. JONES [1921–1965]

Poem

The hand that dreams of poems by my side
My violent friend who dreams me in the dark
Blood-spilling down the pathways of the stars
Seed-scattering in many a summer field
Could conquer kingdoms, burn tall cities down
Or lay a benediction on the breasts
Of her who lies so white and dreamless in my sleep.

What is the monstrous imagining
That could so move this curved and passionate friend
To such tall deeds? what is the hidden metre
That moves these crooked bones? what song
Sings in the nerves and moans along the blood
Impelling them to vast and prodigal deeds?

Only the slim curved whiteness of the hands
The bones' strength and the sensitive finger-tips
Whorled round their mystery, revealing nothing
Can spell the answer in a frantic scribble
Or in curved gentleness around her breasts.

My passionate ally dreaming at my side
Conceiving poems in the chapelled dark
Apocalyptic fingers grasping stars

And scattering their seed across the summer
White hand, curved hand, o dreaming hand
Be always passionate for me, and dream
Me poems down the pathways of the stars.

MICHAEL AYRTON [1921–1975]

You canting kestrel streaming down the sky

You canting kestrel streaming down the sky
Plummet and screaming quit your cherished height
In anguish. Oh Apollo, lidless eye
Who gives all sight to creatures, mark her plight
And smile upon her passage as you fill
The bowl of morning with your gilded spite.
Go, stalk your apex, yawning as you spill
Your phoenix gold upon her and your might.
Lean on her back and drive her down the sky
Weigh down her wings with all your weight of light.
I come to match you. Icarus can fly
To combat with a burning god in flight.

Icarus flies to tear the furnace wind,
Climbs the steep sky to hawk the lowering sun
And tread upon his malice. I am finned
To swim the flooding sun-shoal in my run.
My scream shall cause the molten sky to shake:
Fall, kestrel, from your haven in the wind,
You lizard bird who tumble in my wake,
Fall as you scream and splinter up your scream
And seek the shadow's comfort and the lake
Of darkness under mountains. In the stream

Of hungry heat the god pours out, I take
The source of my ascent towards my dream.

And so I took the bees from the little box

And so I took the bees from the little box in which they had been brought. I killed each one with a needle and gutted it with the sharpest of my knives and I did so with as much reverential care as a priest would sacrifice seven bulls to Zeus. I mantled each fragile carapace and burnt it out of the mantle and, making each laborious insect laboriously immortal, I poured gold into these tiny moulds. When, many hours later, I broke them open there were seven bees of solid gold. Each wing and every leg perfect, they lay on the palm of my hand.

'Here in your honour, Artemis', I said, 'the most fragile sacrifice ever made you. Each victim ritually killed, each pyre ritually kindled and behold, each is a votive to last forever'. And I fastened the bees upon the comb so that they seemed to be coming and going about their sacred business without which no man could cast the bronze doors of a temple to Apollo nor make any bronze sculpture.

It had been many hours of work, for all had minutely to be accomplished, all blurring of the cast chased out and burnished. I lay down by the bench and slept as the charcoal cooled in my kiln, and had no dreams nor remembered any grief.

ROY PORTER [1921–2006]

from *Walk to Departure: IV*

As I happened by chance upon the mountain
Hearing an aeroplane to look up into the sky
I saw the light like a jasper stone
Descending out of heaven clear as crystal.
I watched its self-conception on the water
And its affirmation along the edge
Of the knife with which you were cutting bread:

> Yes, we have subdued the knife
> As we have tamed the horse and bull
> There is no more mana in the blood of the bull
> There is no slaying in the knife.

I remarked concisely on the light,
You answered as I had expected
And our bright talk grew rankly
Between our lips over your eyes and hair
Until the palaces that every motion
Of your body and thoughts were building
Rose hidden from me with Angkor in the forest.

I kissed you as you had expected;
Your lips were warm, the poison of the thermos draught
Yet hung on them, which was the second death.

R.L. COOK [1921–2004]

To Those Who Build

Print all the waste lands with the ploughman's boot,
Mellow the atlas with unending sheaves;
Carpet the desert with a sward of leaves:
Let every barren husk grow fat with fruit.

And surge the tide of plenty through the caves
That pock the towns with poverty and filth,
Channelled by blue-print and controlled by wealth,
To purge the foulest alley with its waves.

Then sweep the wing of culture through the skies
Over the men who, recreating Eden,
Will eat, unpunished, apples as they redden
And find an Eve who waits with guiltless eyes.

But still there will be agony to bear
Upon the mind: for see – the child that weeps
Today and here weeps always, everywhere,
And through the man the endless echo creeps:

And though the earth spreads perfect, evergreen
And everyman's a king, yet there will be
The shadow of that agony between
The fevered flesh and tomb's tranquillity.

DRUMMOND ALLISON [1921–1943]

Dedication

Had there been peace there never had been riven
Asunder my humility and pride,
My greed and patience. Had I not accepted
The gift of sin I never had been shriven.

Had I not met and missed you in the room,
Had I not lost your body and your leisure,
I had not learned I could dispense with love
Like a blind man unhindered by the gloom.

For a Medical Student, Against Death

Jokers and lovers try to outflank truth
Each bound to find the depth of its defence;
Women with Gods and poets with a myth
Never discover fictions fierce like facts.

But hearing fearlessly official speakers
Revealing our antagonist's no wraith
Indeed you can ignore the evil omen,
Stamp on His envoys, rip His worthless pacts.
Carrying bones and books to guard your youth,
Oh! end the truce that chills us with suspense,
Even in vain assault the impregnable walls of Death.

PHILIP LARKIN [1922–1985]

Sonnet

Flesh to flesh was loving from the start,
But only to itself, and could not calm
My skeleton of glass that sits and starves,
Nor my marsh hand that sets my music out:

It is not kissing at the acid root
Where my bald spirit found a crying home,
Nor my starved blood that your excitement loves,
And wears all brilliant badged upon your coat:

Yet hand will praise, and skeleton delight,
And root will kiss, and spirit hold you warm,
And blood will call you blood and wear your lives
All red and blue and golden on its heart.

***

But you are far away and I have grown
A sack of fever hanging from the sun.

IAN BANCROFT [1922–1996]

Three Poems (For Corinna): III

Storm sweeping. Hands cold and eyes
Shuttered against the hail; feet finding
Rock, no road, they read their lives
Printed in blocked stone by lightning.

Power possessed them, lost by the lake;
Not strength but suffering; over the pass
Snow-cairned and corniced by the rock
Their Capitol. Nails scarred the moss.

Wind on the summit; brows blind
And no screes sensing: the hanging rock,
Last breath, and falling falling. One sound,
Stone-sighing, closed their Sibylline Book.

Bridge on the Orne, 1944

Somewhere in the soft heart of this chaos
Hides a deliberate hand of childlike shyness
Which sent us off despairing to the bridge.

June's tenderness lies gently on the river,
Nettles climb crazily amongst the idiotic
Jungle of twisted gliders. A tank burns, crackling.
Dead horses, swelling already, wear new blinkers
Of foraging flies mauling their latest plunder.
And over the narrow sorrel field, scorched black
By smoke and fire, rises the sniping wood.
A cow spread fancifully half on the bank

Thrusts four grotesque legs into the tangle
Of careless briar. Look at its eyes
Staring under the water like a pathetic pike,
Some angler's triumph in a beer-cool parlour.
And in a patchwork, like the second coming,
Men sprawl about the grass, their faces grey,
And hands flung outwards, hooked fingers clutching
At some unknowable vision. See how the palms
Shine pink and moist still, and the rim of dust
Clings to the dry mouths. One there was weeping,
White runnels on his dusty cheek trace out
His few last tears, for he was very young.

Now there is only fear and wonder,
Disgust perhaps will come tomorrow, when the heat
Puffs out decay like invisible smoke rings;
But now we look at the fatal wood, watching green branches
For movement in the windless afternoon.
A butterfly settles lightly on this man's temple,
White on dark red, then flies away.
We lose it against the blinding golden sun.

SIDNEY KEYES [1922–1943]

Elegy for Mrs Virginia Woolf

Unfortunate lady, where white crowfoot binds
Unheeded garlands, starred with crumpled flowers,
Lie low, sleep well, safe from the rabid winds
Of war and argument, our hierarchies and powers.

Let the clear current spare you, once
A water spirit, spare your quiet eyes;
Let worm and newt respect your diffidence –
And sink, tired lovely skull, beyond surprise.

Over that head, those small distinguished bones
Hurry, young river, guard their privacy;
Too common, by her grave the willow leans
And trails its foliage fittingly.

In time's retreat, a stickleback's
Most complicated house, she lies:
Colours and currents tend her; no more vex
Her river-mind our towns and broken skies.

All Souls: A Dialogue: II: The Stranger

O otherwise than gently
The wind blows in your country.
I am the unborn lonely
Image of your destiny.

No portent goes before me,
No star; no virgin bore me.

But you dare not deny me
Conjure nor defy me.

You may not tip the arrow
With silver, exorcise me;
You may not pluck the yarrow
Against me, set the mask
At your heart's door, despise me
Or refuse what I ask.

Glaucus

The various voices are his poem now.

Under the currents, under the shifting lights
Of midway water, rolls his fleshy wreck:
Its gurnard eye reflects those airy heights
Where once it noted white Arcturus set.

Gull-swift and swerving, the wet spirit freed
Skims the huge breakers. Watching at the prow
Of any southbound vessel, sailor, heed
Never that petrel spirit, cruel as pride.

Let no cliff-haunting woman, no girl claim
Kinship with Glaucus, neither sow
The tide with daffodils, nor call his name
Into the wind, for he is glorified –
And cold Aegean voices speak his fame.

War Poet

I am the man who looked for peace and found
My own eyes barbed.
I am the man who groped for words and found
An arrow in my hand.
I am the builder whose firm walls surround
A slipping land.
When I grow sick or mad
Mock me not nor chain me:
When I reach for the wind
Cast me not down:
Though my face is a burnt book
And a wasted town.

GLORIA KOMAI [BORN 1922]

Initial

You call us winter fools. You do not know
That underground uneasily we sleep,
Pierced by presentiment, sharp startled cry
Of wind awaking echo. Blind and sure
We feel our wary inches. Syllables
Knock indistinct, the sparrow housekeeping.
We persevere, as some pursue a star.

Earth cracks like thunder; we are struck by sight
Like lightning. Book of world, the brown page turns,
Bright green ink punctuates, the sun exclaims,

Days flow like lines and summer is a verse
Set down. Remember us, the priests who pray
In your temples, the first snowdrops who break
The frozen crust of earth, who give your Word.

KINGSLEY AMIS [1922–1995]

My hymn of doves, echoed upon this earth

My hymn of doves, echoed upon this earth
As fast as ears swinging beside the bell,
Lives for a second echoing to birth,
Strikes full on lips reft in a coloured sigh,
Weaves in a skein of tears the distant heart;
Makes us a mountain in a world of sky
And vacant air; the hot blood lashes seed
Unsilting channels in the absent shell.

And soon no pause to wrench us from the act,
No thrusting knife of time between our bodies,
No bawling fear to blow our windows to;
Now fold your pinions, dove, while moons refract
On winter waters and a meantime bed:
The love of angels, menacing the dead.

Something Was Moaning in the Corner

O muskrat, ramble through the living grass
And coil the leaves on the abandoned bone;
Bring to the midden your eliding grease
And load the summer zephyrs with your bane.

O viper, mad with coiling on a pin,
Deadly Narcissus gazing on your scales,
Vomit your naked young sentenced to pain
And learn to love the bad sun where it scalds.

O spider, crawl into my tiny heart
And find your doom. The blood is vacant there.
With needle legs prick my dull skin apart
And build your web of sweet inhuman hair.

Elisabeth at Chamboix

Death is stupid, death is stupid
more than the surviving mind can know,
and its poses are affected
like a dancer's halted in their flow.

Hard to trace the form of Adam
in a heap of sacking blown with gas;
hard to credit with sensation
source of midden odours that will pass.

These have found as accidental
what should bring love's utter summary,
nothing in its flash fulfilling.
Nothing is fulfilled by nullity.

See at home the people walking
fascinating, witty in the sun;
clever too, avoiding capture
by the dead, ignorant every one.

And of women you my dearest
most astute to keep your limbs alive,
clear of senseless putrefaction
wisest in your living arts of love.

JACK BEECHING [1922–2001]

Aspects of Love: XIX

Close up your cave, sink in all sinking sea
A momentary rod for finger post,
Engage, compel lava to this long dive;
Blood as a cataract bathe our double ghost.

Moment to pinioned dancer tiptoe swings,
Poised, minuscule, gripping a long high wire
Pole like compelling pinions, wings, o sun
Support, transform, the rigid, leaping flyer.

Close up becomes incorporate, the cave
A diver's bell, a stonesthrown, sinking ball
Rolling down bed of ocean, drowned with blood
Streaming from ears, mouth, icy waterfall.

Streaming from eyes like weeping jettisoned
On other eyes too deadly close for sight.
Close up your sinking sigh, o momentary
Cave, cataract, sea bed bursting with sunlight.

JOHN WALLER [1922–1995]

Nigel

Nigel drowning in summer has heart's treasure,
Sun joy on flesh, sorrow surging of sea,
Sand loose below free body, pale brown
The skin rippling with long loosing
Of city breath, sea swell
Brave in the ear, all well
In this dear kingdom.

Enough for a day? Enough, Nigel, for life.
Sun bears deep over sorrow, over the trench
Dawn shows still skin, grey mould over carrion.
Sun rises with no gladness
For no breath. Poor ghost
Thin in the wind, all lost
In this dear kingdom.

DONALD DAVIE [1922–1995]

The Mushroom Gatherers: After Mickiewicz

Strange walkers! See their processional
Perambulations under low boughs,
The birches white, and the green turf under.
These should be ghosts by moonlight wandering.

Their attitudes strange: the human tree
Slowly revolves on its bole. All around
Downcast looks; and the direct dreamer
Treads out in trance his lane, unwavering.

Strange decorum: so prodigal of bows,
Yet lost in thought and self-absorbed, they meet
Impassively, without acknowledgment.
A courteous nation, but unsociable.

Field full of folk, in their immunity
From human ills, crestfallen and serene.
Who would have thought these shades our lively friends?
Surely these acres are Elysian fields.

DENISE LEVERTOV [1923–1997]

Poem

> *'Can we bring heaven nearer than a star,*
> *Or lift the shadow from a world at war?'*
>
> N. Moore

I need a green fluidity of line,
the hills' long contours in my words, to tell
how by unwarranted grace I found this place.

I need the green astonishment of spring,
stillness of music in the mind, to give
the lie to darkness and release the lark.

The green of day assumes in dreams the shade
of eloquence I need, to tell how love
can lay the ghosts of childhood with a smile.

But the ancient lines of mountains break in craters,
destructive skies crack like decaying plaster;
the individual grace is out of place,

and history denies the structure of delight,
contemptuous of its tender vanity;
music refuses to ignore the black confusion of war.

For love must keep silence, remembering poverty's silence;
recalling the ghosts still living and enslaved,
must hide eternity away, and learn
that time engraves upon the prison wall
'spring' as the symbol of a bitter hope.

To the Inviolable Shade

Intimate trivial glow of cigarettes
illumines now the soft striated smoke
gently rising; and murder overhead
knocks at our hearts like an impatient ghost
that batters windowpanes on stormy nights.
Incredible threats grown near as a raised hand
startle familiar dreams to dreaming life,
love on your lips a miracle, and words
magical flowers that bend bright heads to earth.
'Where is tomorrow?' says the pulse of darkness,
'but in the chance fall of a tossed coin?
Time is not master of felicity'.
The pain of the world is in the air we breathe:
you who took stars and sorrow in white arms,
tender satirical lover of the lost,
no pain but your loss can darken all my world.

JOHN ORMOND [1923–1990]

from *Sonnets of the Madonna*

Through the first word of heaven in her head
She hears the death of trees which struck his green
Foliage and parables with their unseen
Touch, miracles curving through drifting blood.
Here is the first recession of the word
From human walls since the bright rainbow's sign
Filled her stunned bone with the approaching grain
Of the blown world when all is harvested.
Hearing the incantation and the kiss
Telling him to the frost before his fruit
Can fall from coming cold to all's last bliss,
She feels the prophetic motion of the root
Start at the dead in dreams, the children wound
Where the prayer touches stone and nurtures ground.

Where the prayer touches stone and nurtures ground
With a torn tongue, she rises to the cry
In the hung heat of his eclipsing sigh,
Mothering sun and night in his dragged wound;
Her son hangs hollow in the blackened towned
Cloud of his waking gospel, swung by
Morning, making his teaching lung burn dry,
Fires in the word twitching the dust on sound.
Her churches topple in the sudden blast
Of his bone from breath, her breath in lasting light,
Rafter and rib in single utterance, lost
To murder burning lust of his blind sight.
The leaves in riot turn thorns into her lids
From the dream-wasting sorrows of his sides.

FRANCIS KING [1923–2011]

The Interval

Birds on the autumn sand
Are motionless as I,
The dead leaf in my hand
Has lost all will to fly:
I am the shore where birds and leaves reposing lie.

Till at some faint alarm
Of wind or voice it heaves
To throw away its calm,
And the bruised mind receives
Its longing back as sky its driven birds and leaves.

PETER HELLINGS [1924–1994]

from *Ceremonies of Bravery: An Exploration of Courage or Variations Upon Valour for the Memory of Fred Riches*

> '… *Nor omitting ceremonies of bravery in the infamy of his nature*'.
> '*What the sun compoundeth, fire analyseth, not transmuteth*'.
> Sir Thomas Browne, *Hydriotaphia*

I

This is a fireman fantasy –
To be read
In the light of funeral pyres, the uneasy
Skeleton of black and red

Twisted, intertwined girders,
Crushed desire
And the amorphous mounds of microscopic murders
Lit by heroic fire.

The first bombs fell like thunder
Without rain,
The dark land echoing with the crash of wonder:
A great blaze in the brain

And the whole town takes fire;
Flaming, a rose
Lights up the enormous skyline of desire:
Axe, helmet and hose

Assume gigantic proportions
In the mind,
Expand to dominate like long dreamed distortions
The desire they defined,

And all unconscious states
Of oppression
And impotence rise like a rabble of secret hates
Long haunting a holy mission.

For the helmet's authority raised
In silhouette
On the skyline of centuries all men have bowed down to and praised
Is transformed to a terrible threat,

And symbolical radiance glows
Upon earth unaware:
The giant axe, the helmet and hundred-foot hose
Stand out in a night of despair.

II

The murderous blade is swung
In great curves
At the doors and windows of houses where wires are strung
Like tautened or severed nerves:

The bright blade splinters wood
And shatters glass
On pavements where the unsplintered children stood
And watched grave people pass.

Now fire bursts like a rose,
And the marriage
Of male and female in the couplings of writhing hose
Grows to a turbulent image

Of impassioned, improdigal desire:
The lust
Of a column of foam to quench an incredible fire
And reduce it to ashes and dust.

For this recurring theme
Of heroes
And heroines is rooted in nightmare and dream:
Axe, helmet and hose

Become the dark images
Of the double
Lives, the conjuror's buried skeleton marriages
Unearthed from the rubble

Of collapsed cathedrals
And halls
Blown to a blazing oblivion of bones and skulls
In a horror of flaming walls

Towering in the terrible hysteria
Of loosened tongues
That confess and condemn in the cells of the interior
Mind where mankind belongs.

III

This is a fireman fantasy
I repeat –
To be read in the glare of disaster in no great heresy;
The fallacy of defeat

Is implicit in flame's delight:
The infernal
Fascination of bravery ablaze in a bitter night
Is not to be made eternal

Nor courage encouraged alone:
For the dread
And the daring of danger is rooted in fibre and bone,
And familiar skies turn red.

What once was admitted joy
May lure
Man to heroic death and utterly destroy
All evidence of allure,

And those who return are aware
Of no fear
Or frenzy of fire in the element they dare,
But always and only the clear

Necessity of essential action
In the heart
Of flame, whose fatal yet fortunate attraction
Drives reason to depart.

For courage is kindled desire
Or the blind
Exaltation of bitterness all murderous deeds inspire
In the dramatic mind

Where bravery burns like a name
In green disguise,
A splendour of spirit tinged with disaster of flame
The ignorant heart denies.

MICHAEL HAMBURGER [1924-2007]

Flowering Cactus: In Memoriam Jankel Adler

Worlds too can be transplanted, alien griefs cry out,
A foreign ecstasy explode in our own house
Or suddenly a desert on the window-sill
Burst into purest red. Great metamorphosis
Which from a shrivelled cactus conjures liquid fire,
Answering absent solitudes and wastes of sky!
Worlds too can wilt; the same green body in whose veins
Visions were stored, sand, water, light were taught to speak
Is parched beyond endurance: yellow now, then brown,
Its flesh hints at no knowledge of potential flowers.

Epitaph for a Horseman

Let no one mourn his mount, upholstered bone
He rode so cruelly over bog and stone,
Log, fence and ditch in every kind of weather;
Nor glibly hint those two came down together:
A horse fell dead and cast his master down,
But by that fall their union was undone.
A broken jade we found, the rider gone,
Leaving no token but his cold clean gear,
Bit, reins and riding-crop for friends to gather.
None but a beast's remains lie buried here.

WILLIAM BELL [1924–1948]

from *Bach Improvising at the Organ*

John, best interpreter of dreams, have pity
on all bewildered men who hear the roar
heaven's orchestra sustains, while yet once more
noon comes like midnight to the eternal city;
Jerusalem with music overflows her
opening throats. Her sun is in eclipse,
hid by his ringing shield the winged composer
numbers her choirs in his apocalypse,
jostling the jangling tendrils of the Gorgon
over her face, till with that overtone
her choirs become enchanted to the stone
nakedness of the turrets of an organ,
jewelled and tall, whose battlements show clear
on distant mountain-tops, about the humming
house of fame, like John's prophetic ear
now heavy with the word, a second coming.

IAN DAVIE [1924–2000]

Landing Party

Darkness with the sigh of love has borne us beyond
The tapered finger, pointing from the lost harbour,
The island's ghost laid on the sea's waiting breast.
Distance is water to the impetus of will
But the shattered spears of the stars on this cold shroud
Woven of mists and cries of the wheeling birds are strewn
As tokens of a defeat too vast for our salt tears –
        Blind gulls and the white crest of lifting waves.

We took no thought for autumn, the trees on the desolate shore,
Patiently awaiting their funeral, with heads unbowed:
And we waited for something also, the death within us
Of something – though not at the relentless wind's decree
Whining now like a wolf as the tide creeps stealthily away
Deserting, whetting its knife in secret haste between
The stinging rocks and the sand in a fury of disregard:
        We could feel almost the shudder of the leaves.

The limbs of the drowned shone bright. Our eyes were hungry
As our knuckles whitened on the bayonet boss and our ears
Grew to caverns of sound. Waiting. Death is a crouching moment
A snapped twig, inch of sound, but life is eternity
And we alone in the midst of it, making the most of nothing.
We who would cry 'Celeriter currite noctis equi'
Disciplined to yell at the opportune moment – but not yet,
        To jab at the straw filled dummy and find it real.

A Dream

I fled in sleep from some imagined harm,
And at the threshold of disaster woke
To hear your gentleness of voice disarm
The heralds of defeat before they spoke.

If you had let them speak, they would have lied;
Yet truth is not so lightly disavowed:
It was the thought that you had left my side
That made me cry my nothingness aloud.

JAMES BERRY [1924–2017]

The Agony

Look how time has gone now
and arrested April tide
circling my good sap in fire
drilling for streams
like no fledgling to be feathered
no bare tree to be leafed
yet rushing to my toes to find no roots
to my head with dead branches
and my good sap's on fire.
What shall I do?
What shall I do?
In what dimension, into what mould
shall I pour the shapes of these
strange forms that haunt me?

ALISON BOODSON [1925–1993]

Poem

The crane against the sky translated steel
into silver; leaves were feathers plucked from
stayed wings of fallen angels: this my heart's flesh,
prisoner in my dungeon-ribs,
my problem-child, my feeble minded brother
I shut away, scourged once nearly to death: –
Suppose I tear the gag out of your mouth,
Unbind your hands and feet and send you forth –
would the light stagger on your darkened eyes?
O, would the streets erupt like buds of lilac,
wrench blossoms out of stone-work, strike your lips
to the responsive fingers – would this key
delight the lock, bring you out into the sun?

WILFRED WATSON [1925–1998]

Emily Carr

Like Jonah in the green belly of the whale
Overwhelmed by Leviathan's lights and liver
Imprisoned and appalled by the belly's wall
Yet inscribing and scoring the uprush
Sink vault and arch of that monstrous cathedral,
Its living bone and its green pulsing flesh –
Old woman, of your three days anatomy
Leviathan sickened and spewed you forth
In a great vomit on coasts of eternity.
Then, as for John of Patmos, the river of life

Burned for you an emerald and jasper smoke
And down the valley you looked and saw
All wilderness becomes transparent vapour,
A ghostly underneath a fleshly stroke,
And every bush an apocalypse of leaf.

And Should She Ask

Of conflagrant Troy tower the flaming stalk
A torch I blossomed in my mother's bowel;
And should she ask what fire burned in her heart,
When in her heart my blood she did distil,
Tell her,
What blood this blood has spilt.

That web of fate which tortured sinful Thebes,
I knotted up within my mother's groin;
And should she ask what sorrowed in her flesh
When in her side my eyes were but blind seeds,
Tell her,
What things these eyes have seen.

Mouth of the mouth that hungered Pharaoh's house,
I was the serpent at my mother's breast;
And should she ask, what at her breast lay there,
When at her pap I eased her of her milk,
Tell her,
What lying mouth her milk did lap.

At crotch of Golgotha, a place of skull,
I was the nail that nailed my mother's bone;
And should she ask what rankled in her womb,
When in her womb my hands lay folded there,
Tell her,
How there ingrew these hangman's hands.

ROBIN SKELTON [1925–1997]

Into Eden: II

In the swerve and circle of the bird,
thwarting its stumbling shadow on the grass,
is the storm that searches us like roots
for living rivers and the pool of peace.

In the thrush's throat is lifting water
under the spring's stone, quick as any child
in leaves of smiles awakening sky and shower
is lofting apple-blossom, white and wild

as caught clouds in a mesh of April boughs
sprigged with sunlight: in the song's cascade
is a searching storm, a growing garden
waking Eden with each Gabriel blade.

from *Patmos: For Margaret, Barbara and John*

Always we dreamt of this. The nothingness
that is the entire has a human face.
We are not lying when we move in love.

Always we come to this. The crystal state
that is the essence burns in human fate.
We are not dying when our passions move.

The Phoenix and the Virgin rise from light,
but wear the red momentum of the blood.

JON SILKIN [1925–1997]

Death of a Son (who died in a mental hospital aged one)

Something has ceased to come along with me.
Something like a person: something very like one.
And there was no nobility in it
Or anything like that.

Something was there like a one year
Old house, dumb as stone. While the near buildings
Sang like birds and laughed
Understanding the pact

They were to have with silence. But he
Neither sang nor laughed. He did not bless silence
Like bread, with words.
He did not forsake silence.

But rather, like a house in mourning
Kept the eye turned in to watch the silence while
The other houses like birds
Sang around him.

And the breathing silence neither
Moved nor was still.

I have seen stones: I have seen brick
But this house was made up of neither bricks nor stone
But a house of flesh and blood
With flesh of stone

And bricks for blood. A house
Of stones and blood in breathing silence with the other
Birds singing crazy on its chimneys.
But this was silence,

This was something else, this was
Hearing and speaking though he was a house drawn
Into silence, this was
Something religious in his silence,

Something shining in his quiet,
This was different, this was altogether something else:
Though he never spoke, this
Was something to do with death.

And then slowly the eye stopped looking
Inward. The silence rose and became still.
The look turned to the outer place and stopped,
With the birds still shrilling around him.
And as if he could speak

He turned over on his side with his one year
Red as a wound
He turned over as if he could be sorry for this
And out of his eyes two great tears rolled, like stones, and he died.

I.R. ORTON [1925–2019]

Because We Both Have Voices

Because we both have voices,
Though mine is weak to sing
Creation's mystery
Or even one face beside us;

Because we walk now
In the nameless streets to see
The birdlike star you found in the high wind;

Because our eyes would sing
And our tongue have visions;
Our glasses stand on the table here, not empty,
But as though we were coming back;

And because we each have voices
There is no exit door that locks behind us,
And no room we enter that will ever lose us.

CHRISTOPHER MIDDLETON [1926–2015]

The Giraffe

With what gentleness
with what extremity of sleep
you observe the world pass
you regard the visitors who watch
your head like a new climate
expecting an apocalypse.

Melancholy and filled
with a wish to die, melancholy
as a living monument, your comic
universe lives only in the savage
and reverberate laughter of
your evening visitors, your only friends.

But if with gentleness
your proud and lovely head should pass
my window and loiter sadly there,
I would touch your cheeks and give
you soft awakening, a piece of bread,
a sign that it is possible to love.

Male Torso

Before I woke, the customed thews
Alighted on strangeness.
Crammed over booms of vine,
The once buxom canvas quilled.

From his hot nest, before I woke,
The snowgoose flew, in skyward rings;
And funnelled air that filled my mouth
Rang with his wingbeat.

The customed eyes, before I woke, were glass:
A bleating queen whose legs were sheaths
Of hammered moon fed swill to pigs;
With needle oars they swept her bark

Through floes of starfruit, dolphins cutting
Under her eyelid's bow blue arcs in air;
And the beat of her oars like drums
Fanned my hushabye head.

Before I woke, no savour was;
But three birds sang that song they piped as girls,
Of sweetness, golden-rinded, and the fountaintree,
For mortal grapes cooled in my hands.

Then down the quartz-walled galleries of ears I coiled,
Before I woke; cymbals clashing sliced their hill,
And there with bulls my skew-wigged mother trod
Her crocus dance around its axle;

Counterwheeling Horn and Bear
Shared in her coronal the thud of fingertips on flutes,
Until my customed silence dipped and rose,
And gall was mine and darkness was.

I live now in a hutch of mud,
Without a floor, nailed by the sun,
Now for the interminable writhing sea
A fair food housed in roofless marble.

But if I wake to sniff the air of clustered stars,
I'm clothed in dew, for babes to drink,
The snowgoose moors her nest on light,
And the small horned worms walk high with hope.

ELIZABETH JENNINGS [1926–2001]

Lazarus

It was the amazing white, it was the way he simply
Refused to answer our questions, it was the cold pale glance
Of death upon him, the smell of death that truly
Declared his rising to us. It was no chance
Happening, as a man may fill a silence
Between two heart-beats, seem to be dead and then
Astonish us with the closeness of his presence;
This man was dead, I say it again and again.
All of our sweating bodies moved towards him
And our minds moved too, hungry for finished faith.
He would not enter our world at once with words
That we might be tempted to twist or argue with:
Cold like a white root pressed in the bowels of earth
He looked, but also vulnerable – like birth.

ELLSWORTH MCGRANAHAN KEANE [1927–1997]

Caterpillar

I wonder if
          to die
is any of the things
          they say it is
                    caterpillar…
          butterfly…
          And supposing all
that is of me pupa-prison
          burst
would I
                              caterpillar
                    know myself in wings

from *Fragments and Patterns*

Once the water said
To the wind
I am unwanted
          Need me
I am unplanted
          Seed me
And out of the sweep of the wind's hands
Out of a pattern of tides
Came forth islands

Mountains remember our dawn
And rivers rumble of a time
Before Columbus
Before the bushed beards and red eyes

That spoke of a land long sea-days northward
And the little rippling efforts of memory
That make brows of our blue bays
Know with the wind
Tales of a ghost time's far telling

And time and her captains sailed west
Into a pattern of blood
By a pattern of tides possessed…

Go to, Drake,
Go to, Penn.
Venables, go to.
Rum and blood and the quake
Of a thousand broadsides

(If you would commemorate anything)

Oh Abercrombie rides the flood
Into a pattern of tides
Tides and blood
And the sins of the sea
That may eventually…

This was the temptation:
That they who daring the lips of the ocean
Had found Canaan without benefit of light
Or pillar of cloud
Should bring home the grape
And gorge without thanks

If you see Columbus or Cain
Or Philip of Spain
Tell him…

And this is the condemnation:
That they who gorged grape did not stop to consider
The shock of the vine, that they finding gold
Did not stop to consider the rock they had raped
That they making history did not stop to consider
The flesh they had undone...

I talked with the flower
That settled on the silken sea
And the flower said
I know the last brave cacique
Have known him head mountains and eyes tides
Have seen him ripples spreading
Out of tides
And out of a pattern of tides
Islands

And out of a pattern of blood
We
          Oh my islands...

And out of a pattern of tides and blood
History.

CHARLES TOMLINSON [1927–2015]

Poem

Out of the spiralled conch shell
Spill: acorns, over the sleeping thigh;
Over the sleeping thigh: fall
Dreams of crossing oaks.

The wave that knows no breakwater
Washes the land with summer,
The grape rounds to perfection: as
The tide knocks from within.

Wave from the aestival sea
Washes the sleeping thigh,
Crossing oaks loll in the tide,
Acorns cover the sleeping bride.

Acorns cover the sleeping thigh,
Acorns move in a moving tide
Out of the mouth of the dreaming conch-shell,
Barring the washed land with oaks.

The Ballad of Three Dark Angels

Three dark angels said to me:
'The oak, the laurel and the cypress tree –
Plant them in fresh soil', they said,
'And build your house within their shade.

See there grow beside your door
Sunflower, mandrake, hellebore,

Of northern rose and whiter lily
Keeping soil and trellis free.

Rose and lys from time's stalk fade,
Fade, fall, dissolve, put forth no seed.
Where older cultures will not grow
Time is to choose your flowers anew'.

This three dark angels said to me:
'The oak, the laurel and the cypress tree,
Sunflower, mandrake, hellebore
By these dark six set future store'.

ANTHONY CRONIN [1928–2016]

Responsibilities

My window shook all night in Camden Town
Where through the cutting's murk the sibilant engines
Pounded past slowly gasping in the rain.
Three o'clock was a distant clanking sound.

On Primrose Hill the gasfire in my room
Hissed for more money while the sofa bristled.
The unopened wardrobe stared sepulchrally.
It probably was my predecessor's tomb.

Daily I strolled through leaves to look for letters,
A half of bitter or a chance encounter.
My state was ecstasy, illusion, hunger,
And I was often lectured by my betters.

What wonder that I seldom rose till three
When light was leaking from the grimy primrose
That is the western sky of winter London,
Light in the head, lugubrious, cynical, free.

The past, implausible and profitless,
Is yet a part of us, though I suppose
Gide has the right of it: who have no sense
Of their own history know most happiness.

And yet I set that autumn sunlight down,
That delicate, pale ochre and that haze;
My eye so idle and the afternoon
So still and timeless with the haze withdrawn.

I could disown them like a thirties poet.
And yet I set inexplicables down;
And scattered images of London when
With a true love I could most truly know it.

The cavernous Rowtons where the footsteps grew
Unsteadily down each corridor and passed,
The stages marked on all my bootless journeys,
A pub, a railing and a short way through.

I groped through bomb-sites on the Finchley Road,
Fog in the stomach, blanketed in cold.
Next morning when the gears began to groan
Whatever else I had I had no load.

No more than when in Hammersmith one morning
The sun lit up the Broadway through the fog.
Incarnadine, transported I was stalking
Beside the early buses in that dawning.

Nightly the wagons splashed along Watling Street,
Battened down, bound for the pool or for the smoke,
Waiting for lifts I did not know myself,
An avatar, a prehistoric beat.

I saw the landscape of old England like
A man upon the moon, amazing shapes,
Wheels, pulleys, engines, slag-heaps, bricks and dirt,
And furnace sunsets frowning through the smoke.

And heard the poets of old England too
In Watney's pubs repeating cricket scores
And Dylan stories, talk of our medium
And principles and programmes (radio).

The past, predestined, populous and over
Clings in the dampening leaves, the smell of petrol,
On the brown northern heights where I remember
Highgate and Hampstead in a fine October.

BURNS SINGER [1928–1964]

from *Magnificat*

Who then are you
I hazard after?
Are you my love
Who have my love?
I cannot yet decipher you nor disprove.

Where do you lie?
And what between
Us launches this arrogant
Atmosphere
Through which you penetrate like a pointed prayer?

I come to you
Across across,
I come to you
And will be seen
Though five ambiguous senses blaze between.

[…]

I come to you
Across this painful
Noise of my journey
Without a wreath.
I bear no grudge nor cargo. I carry death.

You will surprise
Me at the last.
We two will meet

Where no sun warms,
I, murderer with my body in my arms,

And you with me
As I at last
With you, alive
Past apprehension,
The dizzy annunciation, the slackening tension.

from *The Transparent Prisoner*

They took me somewhere sleeping in the desert
Up middle of a minefield near Benghazi:
And I was hungry – but that was later. At first
It was the Germans – you'd hardly call them Nazi –
Polite and battle-hungry happy men
– O I would like to meet those chaps again.

And everything was decent at headquarters,
After we'd picked our way out like with tweezers,
Decent and capable, and we were ordered
Into small companies, and fed or feasted
Better than back in Cairo. So for ten days
We waited, glad in the shade, glad of delays.

Then we were shifted in a desert truck
Back eighty miles, the sun like liquid steel,
The smell of heat, the nagging – until it took
A hard wrench on my memory to dispel
Those green and English places and the sounds
Which hiccuped at me, festering with old wounds.

But it was still the Germans, and one talked
At great length about his home-town, in what
I soon could recognise as Marburg – talked
And was glad of it, till I let out
A long throng of impatient memories:
Together we mourned the way an instant dies.

There was a Frenchman too – some sort of pilot
In an ugly bandage. The three of us
Got talking, all odd accents, and in a while it
Wasn't just words: we sang the *Marseillaise*,
The *Land of Hope and Glory*, and *Auld Lang Syne*:
Till on that note we reached a little town.

There we changed captors. We were back at base
With I-ties, or Italians, or plain Wops,
Who pinched our watches but could not refuse
To feed us on a diet of their slops.
And it was there that I first learned to sense
The tidy brutality of a barbed-wire fence.

[...]

It must have been two months between the two
Modes of starvation – one, the quick acute
And killing primary need I had come to know.
Death gurgled near it... It seemed a mere brute
Rampant and miserable, plunging with a moan
Its whole weight at me: in me like a bone.

The other – but it was in Germany –
A perilous pedestrian sense of God –
It lasted longer, outlasting sun and snow
Two winters and three summers. I watched the slow plod

Of overladen feet, till I had seen
Footprints like letters form an articulate line.

Or rather – but we lived in a tin hut
With one of those long reaches for a prison
Where the slack landscape folding out of sight
Seems to crop up again behind the horizon;
At least we slept there, when we had got through
With hacking coal for sixteen hours a day.

They kept us there for coal, alive enough
To cut it in the dark, but not to think.
They gave us porridge and a kind of dough
Half-baked to bread, and sticky soup to drink.
I ate it, gave them coal, two years and more,
And shivered in a blanket on the floor.

Any conditions continued long enough
Will stretch themselves until a man can live
All of him, in them; and the lowest life
Give highest impulse headroom, though he have
A hutch, a hole, a hill, to habit, and
Squalor alone to love and understand.

[…]

Lying along my belly, the rock roof
Two feet above, the wet rock floor upon
My muscles sliding, I seemed to grow aloof
From my own body or to grow a skin,
Flesh, form, and senses, deep within my own
And to retire to live in them alone.

My hands against the coal would grow transparent,
Then, like a match felt softly by its flame,
My arms would char into a wandering current;
Warm radiance crept up them till the same
Vivid transparence flooded every part
And I could see the beating of my heart.

As sedentary worms that burrow in
A froth of sand cement it with a slime
Out of their own skin, I too shed my shine
On to the rock below me till in time
It took the same transparence as myself:
I saw its seed, its kernel, through the filth.

[…]

Lying along my belly in the mine,
Or labouring footprints in the German snow,
I, the involved one, learned to love again
And, loving it, attempted to reach through
To the broad air, the people, though for years
My pit-prop prison peopled unawares.

I learned to love the self-same world as now:
For love of it, though its transparency
Was my captivity. I planned carefully how
To reach through to it and in it to be free.
I killed a man. I killed him and escaped
Into it living. Then, at last, I wept.

I got away through the Bohemian South
And into Yugoslavia where I joined
A band of partisans who lived next to death.
In that excitement, thinking was postponed

Or sharpened hard on the best ways to kill.
I kept myself alive, and that was all.

But now as years pass and the war is done
I find myself of evenings often enchanted
And, guessing what goes on within my brain,
Conceive myself as of a being haunted
By corpses more alive than his own flesh:
They dog me with a brittle tenderness

That breaks upon a whim, but nothing breaks
Through my continual sense of loss and sense
Of being cut off by simple slight mistakes,
Everyday errors, from an innocence
That is still mine though it lives a life apart
Folded transparently in the transparent heart.

A Small Grief Has Been Launched

These headlands clench their bare grey talons
Deep into the splash of water, and they scrape
Whitenesses out of waves caught half off-balance
By the burly steadiness of this gaunt cape.

And further out, invisibly exiled there,
Where the full swim of the sea floats salt shoals
Over its bows, under its keel, there rolls
That one small grief, that broken part of prayer.

Of course unseen, naturally, because
The scream of rocks scraping the edge is me.
I am deserted for those anonymous
Regularities of the implacable sea.

Though I can't follow it, though I must
Grasp scant purity from the shallows; although
These stones, my selves, this humid solid dust
That baulks the ocean determines all I know.

There is the grief in exile; somewhere, it
Divides distance, punctuates freedom, soars.
I stand and grasp at water, squat, spit,
Myself my anchor since my selves are shores.

But still the grief, no longer mine, makes free
With every weather and sails on out,
Safe agent, slackened by no rusting doubt
Since it obeys each inch of each decree.

Bound to that wave, it bounds away to this:
Missing, it topples: toppling, is rescued by
The waters of its previous jeopardy:
Directions take it now, a dot of distance.

A dot of distance keeping to its course
Away from me, it rides those changing laws,
This little grief, once mine, now lost in hoarse
Commands that carry it: and yet it draws

The best of me and what I hope to learn
Out into depths these talons cannot reach
And over depths unknown to any speech
Towards shores that dwarf my blind but best concern.

That Autumn Death was talking in the garden

That Autumn Death was talking in the garden
– Not for the first time – but when Spring came round
It didn't stop. Instead, its quiet voice
Kept whispering nothings from the budding ground.

And so, he left the place. At first to Brighton
And drinks and dames and lobsters cooked in wine.
But the sea spat at him. The damp skies glowed
With memories that he took for a sign.

He ran again and reached the south of Spain
In time for almond blossom. Those white flowers
Studded the leafless trees with purity
That drained all pity from the truth it powers.

The woman who possessed him turned to stone.
The olives wrote their stunted message out
Against the sky. The fishermen brought up
Small lean clean things. He hardly dared to doubt.

When he came back he listened. Death was talking
In that soft voice he knew, talking to him.
He answered back and heard the echo calling
Death's name across the garden, suddenly trim.

I said I'd meet you on the other side

I said I'd meet you on the other side
Of all this clutter, and I did set out.

ROSEMARY TONKS [1928–2014]

Running Away

In the green rags of the Bible I tore up
The straight silk of childhood on my head
I left the house, I fled
My mother's brow where I had no ambition
But to stroke the writing
I raked in.

She who dressed in wintersilk my head
That month when there is baize on the high wall
Where the dew cloud presses its lustration,
And the thrush is but a brooch of rain
As the world flies softly in the wool of heaven.

I was a guest at my own youth; under
The lamp tossed by a moth for thirteen winters
Sentenced to cabbage and kisses
By She who crammed an Earth against my feet and
Pulled over me the bright rain
Storm of fleece.

Not for me – citizenship of the backdoor
Where even the poor wear wings; while on Sunday
Gamy ventilations raise their dilettante
In the bonnet of the satin-green dung fly,
And fungus sweats a livery of epaulettes.

I was a hunter whose animal
Is that dark hour when the hemisphere moves
In deep blue blaze of dews
And you, brunette of the birdmusic tree,

Stagger in spat diamonds
Drunkenly.

Like some Saint whose only blasphemy is a
Magnificent juice vein that plucks his groin
With April's coarse magicianship as green
As the jade squirt of fruit, I was the child whose breast
Rocks to a muscle savage as Africa.

Thundercloud, your wool was rough with mud
As the coat of a wild beast on which flowers grow,
Your brogue of grunts so low
They left soil in the mouth. After you, I
Walked as through a Djinn's brain
Gleaming lane.

I was incriminated by your hammer
In my chest. And forfeit to the crepe hoods
Of my mother's eyes; the iron door of her oven
And her church. Skies, cut to blind, had but laid on
Her priest's mouth the green scabs of winter.

But I had the marvellous infection!
Leaning upon my fairy and my dog
In the ultramarine
Latitudes of dew shook like a tear that's carried
Through darkness on the knuckles of
A woman's glove.

I saw each winter where my hen-thrush
Left her fork in famine's white banqueting cloth;
Could I not read as well the tradesman's hand
With its magenta creases – whose soul turns blandly
On a sirloin mattress to smile at the next meal?

O She who would paper her lamp with my wings!
That hour when all the Earth is drinking the
Blue drop of thunder; and in
Dark debris as of a magician's room, my beast
A scented breathing
To the East.

PATRICK CREAGH [1930–2012]

from *do not fail*

do not fail
stealer of sparks
afflicted flint
where my soul strikes

richest ore
deepest mine
genie's lamp
that the dark burns in

when I come smarting
from kind words and smiles
you are my ointments
my soothing oils

TED HUGHES [1930–1998]

Thrushes

Terrifying are the attent sleek thrushes on the lawn,
More coiled steel than living – a poised
Dark deadly eye, those delicate legs
Triggered to stirrings beyond sense – with a start, a bounce, a stab
Overtake the instant and drag out some writhing thing.
No indolent procrastinations and no yawning stares.
No sighs or head-scratchings. Nothing but bounce and stab
And a ravening second.

Is it their single-mind-sized skulls, or a trained
Body, or genius, or a nestful of brats
Gives their days this bullet and automatic
Purpose? Mozart's brain had it, and the shark's mouth
That hungers down the blood-smell even to a leak of its own
Side and devouring of itself: efficiency which
Strikes too streamlined for any doubt to pluck at it
Or obstruction deflect.

With a man it is otherwise. Heroisms on horseback,
Outstripping his desk-diary at a broad desk,
Carving at a tiny ivory ornament
For years: his act worships itself – while for him,
Though he bends to be blent in the prayer, how loud and above what
Furious spaces of fire do the distracting devils
Orgy and hosannah, under what wilderness
Of black silent waters weep.

BRYAN MAGEE [1930–2019]

I have inherited a seed within my veins

I have inherited a seed within my veins
Will bare my bones
And mock my inspiration; a fourth cell
Whose leech lips suck the life-blood from my soul
And dry the beauty from my tender vines.

Now for my sorrow the immediate fire:
Behind the ear
A gaping mouth laughs at my twisted strings
And mute cords, bandaging a dead man's songs
Unsung for ever. I have felt before

This fear, and know that I can never rid
A jagged bud
Upon the world and call it rose: I know
The bud must flower, or a finger's straw
Will stuff the power from the fraying rod.

This is my heritage: the iron seed
Bursts through the shroud
And blossoms in the rock. The sterile stone
Is sprung with flowers. This is my decline,
And this the spear that lacerates my side.

ROY FISHER [1930–2015]

The Lemon Bride

She grew as child, a bitter and perfect fruit,
Her lemon-face, her bewildered goose-glances
Closing on grimy tears, while painfully
Sounded the round bells of her querulous voices.

A time of urine, sunlight and shaking cold,
The dull hair curving like knives about her ears;
Her mind was metal, a power come in too soon,
Ringed thoughts breaking inwards on stumbling fears.

Acid burn iron, lemon to rind-in grief;
So she was perfect, having no world for wrath,
Uncut unharmed, enclosed: in that early pity
So she was child, shaped like a waiting death.

This waxen man, cold as the melon moon,
Ranging abroad, from fire and salt tide free,
Mere thought and earth, in stillness watched by her
And stood about her as a weather tree,

But she was hardened far, beyond his comfort,
No outside weather could nettle or soothe that skin
Nurtured in frost and damp; nor might caresses
Make any path for calm love to come in.

Smooth as a creamy stone or a sea-worn bough,
He stayed impassive, his first forcings gone;
And, stealing her vacant youth, became for her
A wax thought for all pains to fasten on.

And when she knew him with her, the shuddering girl
Clenched on the bough through hatred; her grief and rage,
For ever now unleashed from the clinging fruit,
Lashed at the strong master of her undreamed age.

She kept under savage daylight her still-blind womb,
Still lemon womb; and a scattered soundless rain
Opened her shifting world, where a dark sky shadowed
Great figures, ominous, comforting, tall beyond pain.

Double Morning

This long inconstant waking to a day
Hung round with clouds, fouled with dark smears of rain
          On passive walls of grey
That spent-out gusts obscurely trouble,
Makes a contented window, whose wide pane
Looks two ways on a world made double;
Uncertain day, uncertain dream.

I wake under wings, among such wraps
As yield to dawn's murk imperceptibly;
          My limbs succeed to histories that lapse
Slow-fingered into the giant holes of night,
From their persuasions loosing me,
Comforted in this ashen world to remember them:
Dreams of an unknown freedom and appetite.

For I have been through and still am moist from it
Some place of birth in that last untroubled plain of sleep:
          A misted, populous marl-pit
          Where the body's made whole;
And countless human limbs lie folded deep,

Growing in ease under a silvered rain,
In dream-earth's strange and common bowl
Denuded of identity and pain.

Morning's cold glass lights my hand;
My own corpse fingers moving in a bed
        Feel on my flesh a shingle strand
That sea scrubs under sleeping and half-awake;
Touches that call back signs from the mothering dead
Whose secret forms and rest I shared
Before their soft revival at this daybreak.

Washed clear like streets of shores after a storm,
I take my colours only from gulls and shells.
        This love need not grow warm,
But rests as winter soil under my thoughts
And will upon my living flesh lie so
After day's riding edge dispels
The dream's mist and the dawn's uncertain window.

TONY CONNOR [BORN 1930; LIVES IN THE USA]

from *The Seven Last Poems from the Memoirs of Uncle Harry*

Gone lad gone in the blinding brine,
        I've a racing tide to face
        and the wrath of God's in the bang
        and no breath for past love
love of the all but last towering heartbreaker.
O soon for me the falling beyond care
        of any and every pieced
        and patched hulk of song;
        after:– only the fierce
waters over the split heart the caved mind.

And none to say farewell; not one
        of the many I made from strutting
        storm on imagined sea
        or dumb in the brightest light
and dappled blue deceit of incredible summer.
Let it be death without words, and more
        than silence: the absolute
        hardly deserved mercy
        of an unconceived street;
that never-mouth before absence began.

Elegy for Alfred Hubbard

Hubbard is dead, the old plumber;
who will mend our burst pipes now,
the tap that has dripped all the summer,
testing the sink's overflow?

No other like him. Young men with knowledge
of new techniques, theories from books,
may better his work straight from college,
but who will challenge his squint-eyed looks

in kitchen, bathroom, under floorboards,
rules of thumb which were often wrong;
seek as erringly stopcocks in cupboards,
or make a job last half as long?

He was a man who knew the ginnels,
alleyways, streets – the whole district,
family secrets, minor annals,
time-honoured fictions fused to fact.

Seventy years of gossip muttered
under his cap, his tufty thatch,
so that his talk was slow and clotted,
hard to follow, and too much.

As though nothing fell, none vanished,
and time were the maze of Cheetham Hill,
in which the dead – with jobs unfinished
waited to hear him ring the bell.

For much he never got round to doing,
but meant to, when weather bucked up,
or worsened, or when his pipe was drawing,
or when he'd finished this cup.

I thought time, he forgot so often,
had forgotten him, but here's Death's pomp
over his house, and by the coffin
the son who will inherit his blowlamp,

tools, workshop, cart, and cornet
(pride of Cheetham Prize Brass Band),
and there's his mourning widow, Janet,
stood at the gate he'd promised to mend.

Soon he will make his final journey;
shaved and silent, strangely trim,
with never a pause to talk to any-
body: how arrow-like, for him!

In St Mark's Church, whose dismal tower
he pointed and painted when a lad,
they will sing his praises amidst flowers
while, somewhere, a cellar starts to flood,

and the housewife banging his front-door knocker
is not surprised to find him gone,
and runs for Thwaite, who's a better worker,
and sticks at a job until it's done.

PETER REDGROVE [1932–2003]

Lazarus and the Sea

The tide of my death came whispering like this
Soiling my body with its tireless voice.
I scented the antique moistures when they sharpened
The air of my room, made the rough wood of my bed, (most dear),
Standing out like roots in my tall grave.
They slopped in my mouth and entered my plaited blood
Quietened my jolting breath with a soft argument
Of such measured insistence, untied the great knot of my heart.
They spread like whispered conversations
Through all the numbed rippling tissues radiated
Like a tree for thirty years from the still centre
Of my salt ovum. But this calm dissolution
Came after my agreement to the necessity of it;
Where before it was a storm over red fields
Pocked with the rain and the wheat furrowed
With wind, then it was the drifting of smoke
From a fire of the wood, damp with sweat,
Fallen in the storm.

I could say nothing of where I had been,
But I knew the soil in my limbs and the rain-water
In my mouth, knew the ground as a slow sea unstable
Like clouds and tolerating no organisation such as mine
In its throat of my grave. The knotted roots
Would have entered my nostrils and held me
By the armpits, woven a blanket for my cold body
Dead in the smell of wet earth, and raised me to the sky
For the sun in the slow dance of the seasons.
Many gods like me would be laid in the ground
Dissolve and be formed again in this pure night

Among the blessing of birds and the sifting water.
But where was the boatman and his gliding punt?
The judgment and the flames? These happenings
Were much spoken of in my childhood and the legends.
And what judgment tore me to life, uprooted me
Back to my old problems and to the family,
Charged me with unfitness for this holy simplicity?

GEOFFREY HILL [1932–2016]

Genesis

I

Against the burly air I strode
Crying the miracles of God.

And first I brought the sea to bear
Upon the dead weight of the land;
And the waves flourished at my prayer,
The rivers spawned their sand.

And where the streams were salt and full
The tough pig-headed salmon strove,
Ramming the ebb, in the tide's pull,
To reach the steady hills above.

II

The second day I stood and saw
The osprey plunge with triggered claw,
Feathering blood along the shore,
To lay the living sinew bare.

And the third day I cried: 'Beware
The soft-voiced owl, the ferret's smile,
The hawk's deliberate stoop in air,
Cold eyes, and bodies hooped in steel,
Forever bent upon the kill'.

III

And I renounced, on the fourth day.
This fierce and unregenerate clay,

Building as a huge myth for man
The watery Leviathan,

And made the long-winged albatross
Scour the ashes of the sea
Where Capricorn and Zero cross,
A brooding immortality –
Such as the charmed phoenix has
In the unwithering tree.

IV

The phoenix burns as cold as frost;
And, like a legendary ghost,
The phantom-bird goes wild and lost,
Upon a pointless ocean tossed.

So, the fifth day, I turned again
To flesh and blood and the blood's pain.

V

On the sixth day, as I rode
In haste about the works of God,
With spurs I plucked the horse's blood.

By blood we live, the hot, the cold,
To ravage and redeem the world:
There is no bloodless myth will hold.

And by Christ's blood are men made free
Though in close shrouds their bodies lie
Under the rough pelt of the sea;

Though Earth has rolled beneath her weight
The bones that cannot bear the light.

SYLVIA PLATH [1932–1963]

The Dead

Revolving in oval loops of solar speed,
Couched in cauls of clay as in holy robes,
Dead men render love and war no heed,
Lulled in the ample womb of the full-tilt globe.

No spiritual Caesars are these dead;
They want no proud paternal kingdom come;
And when at last they blunder into bed
World-wrecked, they seek only oblivion.

Rolled round with goodly loam and cradled deep,
These bone shanks will not wake immaculate
To trumpet-toppling dawn of doomstruck day:
They loll forever in colossal sleep;
Nor can God's stern, shocked angels cry them up
From their fond, final, infamous decay.

DANIEL HUWS [BORN 1932; LIVES IN WALES]

Sons of Men

Past dawn, past cockcrow, into the bright of day
They slumber on, hustled by morning's clamour
Never so far as to outrange the choice
Of the blissful slither back to annihilation.
Sleep, motherly sleep, clasp your sons
Till their eyelids spring open in surfeit; then as they scatter –
Defeated men, your matrix dark in their minds –
The rest of their ruined day you need fear no rival.

INDEX OF POETS

An asterisk denotes a contributor to the series of three Apocalyptic anthologies, all edited by J.F. Hendry and Henry Treece: *The New Apocalypse: An Anthology of Criticism, Poems and Stories* (Fortune Press, 1940); *The White Horseman: Prose and Verse of the New Apocalypse* (Routledge, 1941); and *The Crown and the Sickle: An Anthology* (Staples Press, 1944).

The contents pages record dates of birth and death, where known. The source from which the text of the poem has been taken is also recorded, not necessarily the first publication; where the poem was written at a significantly earlier date, this appears before the publication data.

Biographical notes seem unnecessary. It is indeed fitting to be known that Ian Bancroft, a contributor to the third Apocalyptic anthology, served in WWII as a captain from Normandy to the Rhine, then joined the Civil Service, of which he became head, until his ennoblement, as Lord Bancroft of Coatham, after constant clashes with Margaret Thatcher. With Google to hand, however, most of the information that might have been supplied is readily obtainable.

INDEX OF TITLES